ADAM STRATMEYER

Psychological Theories of Personality

A Practical(ish) Guide for the Layperson

Dedicated to Jennifer, who always knew that life's true color, much like space, is black, revealing the stars more brilliantly.

Contents

Introduction

Hi, Thank you much for deciding to join me on what's shaping up to be quite the adventure. As I forge ahead on what is blossoming into a series, my mission remains unswervingly clear: to kindle a flame of inspiration within others, mirroring the very spark that set me on my own path. My voyage across diverse intellectual terrains, especially in the realm of personality theories, has been propelled not by an expertise claimed, but by a fervent passion and reverence for these disciplines. These fields, with their intricate mosaics of concepts and personas, have not only ensnared my fascination but also that of many comrades along the way.

In my time dabbling in undergraduate psychology, I've stumbled upon a curious phenomenon. The topic of personality theories, whether it's a casual chat or a deep dive, always seems to light a fire under folks, echoing a thought I've had and heard from many: "Maybe I should scribble down my own Theory of Personality." This little nugget of ambition, as humble as it might sound, peels back the curtain on a truth. It shows just how enticing this field is, beckoning us all to leave our mark.

As I roll out this first edition, I'm well aware it might not be perfect—perhaps leaning a bit too much into personal tales or ambitiously broad in scope. My goal? To maybe find that sweet spot between sharing engaging stories and providing solid, digestible content, blending scholarly chat with a dash of personal touch. As you wander through these pages, consider this an open invite to join the conversation. Share your thoughts, poke holes, offer praise—it's all in the name of polishing future editions.

A heartfelt thanks for your curiosity, patience, and willingness to dive into this exploration with me. I hope this book not only expands your knowledge of personality theories but also ignites a lasting fascination with the rich tapestry of the human mind.

Special thanks are due to Dr. James McReynolds, for introducing me to the profound concept of tragedy and guiding me through these theories. Jessica Jensen for her support, and inspirational thirst for knowledge, and to Nicole, for the simple yet heartfelt hand-drawn sketches that grace the beginning of each chapter. Nicole's generosity was extended while caring for her newborn son, which adds a unique touch to this work.

YHS, As Always,

Adam Ian Stratmeyer JD

Historical Overview

When I first ventured into the realm of personality theories, my expectations leaned towards a more hands-on, experimental approach. However, I found myself embarking on a historical journey, which was crucial for a comprehensive understanding of the field. This journey, first taken during my academic studies and later revisited during grad school, was akin to an unintended, yet profound, history class in psychology. Let's delve deeper into this rich history, marking key milestones and their impact on our understanding of human personality.

Wilhelm Wundt and Structuralism (1870s): Our story begins with Wilhelm Wundt, who established the first psychology laboratory in Leipzig, Germany, in 1879, a seminal event in the history of psychology (Schultz & Schultz, 2016). Structuralism, spearheaded by Wundt and later by Edward Titchener, sought to dissect the mind's structure through introspection (Titchener, 1901-1905). This approach laid the foundational stones for experimental psychology.

William James and Functionalism (1890s): William James, often hailed as the father of American psychology, introduced Functionalism in the 1890s, challenging the narrow focus of Structuralism (James, 1890). James emphasized studying the functions of consciousness and how it aids adaptation to environments, broadening psychology's scope to encompass learning, development, and personality.

Sigmund Freud and Psychoanalysis (1890s): The late 1890s saw the rise of Sigmund Freud's Psychoanalysis, a groundbreaking development in psychology. Freud proposed the existence of the unconscious mind and its influence on behavior, introducing concepts like the id, ego, and superego (Freud, 1900). His theories provided a novel lens for understanding human personality and its development.

John B. Watson and Behaviorism (1913): The focus shifted to observable behavior with John B. Watson's introduction of Behaviorism in 1913, which posited that behavior is learned and subject to environmental influences (Watson, 1913). B.F. Skinner later expanded this school, emphasizing operant conditioning and its role in shaping behavior (Skinner, 1938).

Humanistic Psychology (1950s): The mid-20th century saw the emergence of Humanistic Psychology as a "third force" in psychology. Pioneers like Carl Rogers and Abraham Maslow advocated for a holistic understanding of the person, focusing on self-actualization and personal growth (Rogers, 1951; Maslow, 1954). This movement arose as a response to the perceived limitations of both Psychoanalysis and Behaviorism.

Cognitive Psychology (1960s): A resurgence of interest in mental processes led to the advent of Cognitive Psychology in the 1960s, examining internal mental processes like memory, thinking, and problem-solving (Neisser, 1967). This field brought new understanding to how we process information and respond to our environment.

Current Perspective (21st century): Despite various models' emergence, the medical model still holds significant influence in mental health treatment, treating mental disorders akin to physical illnesses (Ghaemi, 2009). However, its tendency to oversimplify the complex tapestry of human psychology is notable. In response, the biopsychosocial model was developed, integrating biological, psychological, and social factors for a holistic understanding of mental health and personality (Engel, 1977). This model, while inclusive, is not without limitations, reflecting psychology's ongoing struggle to find a unified approach to understanding the human mind and behavior.

Psychology, as a discipline, is continuously evolving. As we explore various personality theories, we do so understanding that the field is grappling with its identity and methodologies. This exploration is not just about academic knowledge but also about appreciating the discipline's depth and breadth, recognizing the need for ongoing critique and evolution.

The Inescapable Great Man Theory

When delving into the annals of history and psychology, one inevitably stumbles upon the Great Man Theory. To write a book of this nature without addressing it would be like discussing the ocean without acknowledging water. However, this isn't to imply that I fully endorse the Great Man (or Great Woman or Great Person) Theory of history. Yes, it's undeniable that history is peppered with remarkable individuals whose contributions have shaped our world. But, is it solely their inherent greatness, or were they just at the right place at the right time?

Consider Sigmund Freud. He made groundbreaking strides, discovering the stimulating effects of cocaine and the therapeutic power of simply letting people talk about their feelings. While these were indeed revolutionary at the time, one can't help but ponder: were these ideas merely byproducts of being in positions of power and influence? This isn't to downplay Freud's contributions, but rather to contextualize them within the broader tapestry of history and circumstance.

My deterministic view inclines me to believe that many historical figures were products of their time and place. This perspective doesn't diminish their work but rather situates it within a larger narrative where context plays a crucial role. The Great Man Theory does hold merit, but it often becomes redundant and tiresome to constantly focus on "so many old, dead white guys" in a seemingly endless parade.

In this work, I aim to strike a balance. I strive to place the theory and concept above the individual, to focus on the ideas rather than the myths that surround the personages. However, it's a challenging tightrope to walk, as the allure of the 'Great Man' in history is strong and often romanticized.

The Great Man Theory, initially proposed by Thomas Carlyle in the 19th century, posits that history is largely shaped by the actions of great men, whose personal attributes and abilities destine them for greatness (Carlyle, 1841). Carlyle argued that these individuals possess unique qualities that set them apart and enable them to have a disproportionate impact on history. This view, however, has been critiqued for its overemphasis on individual agency, often at the expense of acknowledging broader social, cultural, and historical forces (McLellan, 1997).

The more we examine personality theories, it's essential to recognize the interplay between individual brilliance and the context that nurtures or suppresses it. The stories of these 'great men' and women are not just about their personal journeys but also about the societies, cultures, and historical moments that shaped their paths.

In conclusion, while the Great Man Theory offers a lens to view history, it's not without its limitations. It's a narrative that captures our imagination, celebrating individual achievement and heroism. However, it's equally important to acknowledge the broader forces at play – the unseen currents that shape the course of history. As you journey through this book, I encourage you to consider both the individual and the context, the person and the theory, and how they intertwine to weave the rich tapestry of psychological thought.

Interdisciplinary Perspectives

In delving into the world of psychology, and particularly in the study of personality, it becomes apparent that segregating psychology from its interdisciplinary connections is not just impractical, but almost impossible. Psychology, initially emerging from the broader field of medicine, has long extended its influence, integrating insights from philosophy, sociology, economics, biology, physics, and chemistry. This convergence is vital for a comprehensive understanding of the human psyche.

Wilhelm Wundt, often hailed as the father of modern psychology, embarked on his pioneering work in Leipzig with an ambition to understand commonalities in human thought (Boring, 1950). His investigations, although rooted in psychology, transcended into the realms of philosophy and biology. This exemplifies the interconnectedness of various disciplines, a theme that remains pertinent in contemporary psychological studies.

My journey as an educator, traversing the realms of biology, psychology, and sociology, has highlighted the seamless fusion of these disciplines in understanding human behavior and cognition. Each discussion about one invariably intersects with the others, revealing an intricate mosaic of human understanding. This interconnectedness raises awareness of the knowledge gaps we might harbor, underscoring the importance of a multidisciplinary approach.

Wundt's legacy in psychology is a testament to the interdisciplinary nature of the field. His work laid the foundation for various psychological schools of thought, each drawing from and contributing to different fields. For example, the behaviorist approach, initiated by John B. Watson, was deeply influenced by earlier works in physiology and philosophy (Watson, 1913). Similarly, the development of psychoanalysis by Sigmund Freud brought together insights from neurology and the emerging field of psychiatry (Freud, 1917).

The integration of sociology into psychological understanding is equally critical. Émile Durkheim's work on social factors affecting individual behavior laid the groundwork for social psychology, bridging the gap between individual and societal phenomena (Durkheim, 1897). This blending of sociology and psychology is crucial in understanding how societal structures impact individual personality development.

In modern times, the advent of cognitive psychology brought forth an integration of computer science and neuroscience. The cognitive revolution of the 1950s and 1960s, with pivotal figures like George Miller and Noam Chomsky, drew parallels between the human mind and computer processing, leading to a richer understanding of human thought and language (Miller, 1956; Chomsky, 1959).

In my teaching and lecturing experiences across biology, psychology, and sociology, the interconnectedness of these disciplines consistently emerges. Discussing one invariably leads to overlaps with the others, emphasizing how intertwined our understanding of the human condition is with various fields of study. This book aims not just to be a treatise on psychology but a broader exploration of the philosophy of personality. After all, many of the great thinkers in this field held doctorates in philosophy, not just psychology (Kusch, 1995).

This multidisciplinary approach is crucial for a holistic understanding of personality. It's not just about psychological theories but also about the philosophical, biological, sociological, and even economic contexts that shape these theories. As we delve deeper into the theories of personality, let us keep in mind this rich tapestry of interdisciplinary insights, for they are the threads that weave together a more complete picture of the human psyche.

The evolution of psychological thought is deeply enmeshed with advancements in various disciplines. For instance, the development of humanistic psychology in the mid-20th century, championed by figures like Carl Rogers and Abraham Maslow, was not just a psychological phenomenon. It was also a reflection of broader cultural and philosophical shifts towards individualism and self-actualization (Rogers, 1951; Maslow, 1954). This movement underscored the importance of personal meaning and self-concept, drawing from existentialist and phenomenological philosophy (Bugental, 1964).

The influence of biological sciences on psychology has been

equally profound. The exploration of the biological basis of behavior and cognition, a key focus of biopsychology, has deepened our understanding of the mind-body connection. The groundbreaking work of Eric Kandel, demonstrating the role of synaptic plasticity in learning and memory, exemplifies the crucial role of biology in shaping psychological theories (Kandel, 2001).

Additionally, the intersection of psychology with economics, particularly in the emerging field of behavioral economics, has revolutionized our understanding of decision-making and rationality. Pioneers like Daniel Kahneman and Amos Tversky challenged the traditional economic notion of the 'rational actor', introducing psychological concepts into economic theory (Kahneman & Tversky, 1979).

Understanding human behavior and personality also demands a sociocultural perspective. The groundbreaking work of Lev Vygotsky on the social origins of cognition illustrates how cognitive development is deeply rooted in a social context (Vygotsky, 1978). His theory of the Zone of Proximal Development emphasized the role of social interaction in learning and development, bridging the gap between individual cognitive processes and the cultural context in which they occur.

The intersection of psychology with anthropology offers another rich vein of insight. The study of cultural variations in psychological phenomena, as explored by figures like Margaret Mead, highlights the diversity of human experience and challenges universalist assumptions in psychology (Mead, 1935).

Looking forward, the field of psychology is poised to become even more interdisciplinary. The integration of artificial intelligence and machine learning in understanding cognitive processes and behavior is a burgeoning area of research. This intersection of psychology with computer science opens new frontiers in understanding human cognition and developing therapeutic interventions (Hassabis et al., 2017).

In neuroethics, the ethical implications of neuroscience discoveries in understanding the human mind are being explored, merging ethical and philosophical considerations with neuroscientific research (Farah, 2012).

As we explore the vast landscape of personality theories, it is crucial to keep in mind this interdisciplinary richness. Psychology is not just a standalone field but a tapestry woven from many threads – philosophical, biological, sociological, economic, and more. This tapestry provides a more nuanced, holistic view of human nature and behavior.

In this book, my endeavor is to present not just a psychological perspective but an interdisciplinary one, reflecting the multifaceted nature of human personality. As we delve into the different theories, let us appreciate the various disciplines that contribute to our understanding of the human psyche, recognizing the importance of an integrated approach in psychology.

Note on the the following chapters:

At the beginning of each chapter, the sections titled "front" and "back" serve as compact summaries, designed to fit on a 3x5 note card, capturing the essence of Personality Theory and the chapter's key insights. This approach reimagines the book not as a traditional textbook but as an indispensable reference tool. It is crafted to enhance the reader's educational experience by providing a direct route to understanding, especially appealing to those who prefer clear, brief overviews instead of detailed, lengthy descriptions. By memorizing the information presented in these note card sections, readers can acquire a solid grasp of Personality Theory. The subsequent parts of each chapter offer more detailed discussions and my personal reflections, which, while offering depth, are optional for readers seeking a concise understanding of the concepts. This book is designed to be utilized in a way that aligns with your individual preferences and learning goals, aiming to be both a practical(ish) and enjoyable resource.

Functionalism

Dr. William James, PhD (1890s)

Front

Functionalism Definition: Understanding mental processes by their function in adapting to the environment.

Originator: William James (1890s), pioneer in American psychology.

Analogy:

Car's Functionality = Mind's Adaptive Processes

Riding a Bike = Learning and Adaptation

Fear Response = Functional Emotional Adaptation

Problem-Solving = Adaptation to Challenges

Social Behavior (Cooperation & Competition) = Adaptive Community Living

Goal: Study purposes of mental processes and their practical applications.

Back

Critiques of Functionalism:

Lacks structured methodology.

Broad scope, lacks specificity.

Overlooks biological mechanisms.

Focuses on adaptive functions, neglecting non-functional aspects and abnormal psychology.

William James' Impact: Shifted psychology's focus to practical, functional aspects of mental processes.

Pioneered psychology's academic establishment in the U.S.

Influenced applied psychology and behaviorism.

Legacy and Significance: Critical shift from structural to functional analysis in psychology.

Emphasized real-world application and adaptation of mental processes.

Laid foundations for modern psychological theories and

practices.

Simple Definition of Functionalism

Functionalism in psychology can be likened to understanding a car by observing how it is driven, rather than by examining its individual parts. It's about how mental processes function to enable individuals to adapt to their environment (James, 1890).

Explanation of the Theory

Developed by William James in the 1890s, Functionalism represented a significant shift from the introspective focus of Structuralism to a more practical, application-oriented approach. Functionalism sought to understand the purpose of mental processes and why they exist, rather than just their composition (James, 1890).

Real-World Examples of Functionalism

Learning Through Experience: Riding a Bike

Functionalism delves into how the experience of learning to ride a bike, which involves a series of trials and errors, falling, balancing, and pedaling, contributes to the development of crucial life skills. This process not only teaches physical coordination but also instills confidence and resilience. The act of overcoming the challenge of balancing on two wheels, for instance, is not just about the physical skill; it's about how this skill enables an individual to navigate various environments, from crowded streets to quiet pathways. This example encapsulates Functionalism's focus on understanding how learning through direct experience contributes to an individual's ability to adapt to their surroundings (James, 1890).

Emotional Responses: Understanding Fear

Consider the emotion of fear. From a functionalist perspective, fear is not solely an emotional state but a vital response that has evolved to protect us from harm. When encountering a threatening situation, the experience of fear triggers a series of physiological responses that prepare the body for action – commonly known as the fight-or-flight response. This understanding of fear highlights how our emotional responses are functional adaptations that have evolved to enhance our chances of survival in a potentially dangerous world (James, 1890).

Problem-Solving Skills: Adapting to New Challenges

Functionalism also examines how developing problem-solving strategies is essential for adapting to new and complex challenges. For instance, when an individual faces a difficult task at work, the process of brainstorming solutions, evaluating options, and implementing a plan is not just an intellectual exercise. It's a functional process that enables adaptation to changing environments and circumstances, enhancing the individual's ability to navigate the complexities of modern life (James, 1890).

Social Behavior: The Evolution of Cooperation and Competition

In examining social behaviors, such as cooperation and competition, Functionalism provides insights into how these behaviors have evolved to enable humans to live in communities. Cooperation, for instance, can be seen as a functional adaptation that has enabled collective problem-solving and resource sharing, crucial for the survival of social groups. On the other hand, competition drives individuals to excel and innovate, which can lead to overall advancements for the community. Understanding these behaviors from a functionalist perspective sheds light on how they contribute to the ability of humans to adapt and thrive in diverse social environments (James, 1890).

Critiques of Functionalism

Functionalism, while groundbreaking in its approach to understanding mental processes, has faced several critiques over the years. One of the central criticisms has been its lack of a systematic framework. Unlike its predecessor, Structuralism, which had a clear method in introspection, Functionalism did not offer a similarly structured method for examining mental processes (Leahey, 1992). This lack of a defined methodology made it difficult to replicate and verify Functionalism's findings, a cornerstone of scientific research.

Another significant critique is that Functionalism was considered too broad and diffuse. By attempting to study the purposes of mental processes, Functionalism often spread itself too thin, lacking depth in any one area (Angell, 1907). This breadth, while valuable in creating a more holistic view of mental processes, meant that the theory sometimes lacked the specificity and focus necessary for rigorous scientific inquiry.

Critics also argued that Functionalism often overlooked the underlying mechanisms of mental processes. While it excelled in theorizing about the purposes and functions of mental activities, it did not adequately address how these processes physically and biologically occur in the brain (Blumenthal, 1970). This gap left many questions unanswered, particularly concerning the biological underpinnings of cognition and behavior.

Additionally, some scholars pointed out that Functionalism's focus on utility and adaptation led to a neglect of non-functional aspects of mental life. Not all mental processes have a clear adaptive function, and Functionalism struggled to account for these aspects of human psychology (Hunt, 1993).

Functionalism was also criticized for its limited consideration of abnormal psychology. By focusing predominantly on normal, adaptive mental processes, Functionalism did not thoroughly address mental illness or maladaptive behavior, areas that would later become central to psychological study (Hunt, 1993).

Biography of William James

William James, a figure often playfully remembered for his double-barreled first name, was a trailblazer in bringing psychology to the academic forefront in America. He was the man who introduced psychology into the Ivy League, cementing its status as a discipline worthy of serious academic pursuit (Leahey, 1992). His foray into Functionalism marked a notable departure from Wundt's Structuralism. Where Wundt peered into the mind's structure, James was more intrigued by the role these mental processes played – a kind of 'what are they for' rather than 'what are they made of' approach (James, 1890).

It's important to note that while I may harbor certain reservations about James as an individual, his impact on the psychology landscape, especially in the United States, is undeniable. He had this knack for blending the theoretical with the practical. This wasn't just academic musing for James; it was about understanding how our mental processes helped us navigate the real world. His work paved the way for later developments in applied psychology and behaviorism, fields that would take his ideas about the functionality of the mind and run with them, so to speak (Leahey, 1992).

William James's Functionalism, despite its critiques and limitations, was undeniably a turning point in psychological thought. He shifted the conversation from the structure of mental processes – a bit like looking under the hood of a car – to their purpose and function, akin to understanding why we drive cars and how they change the way we live. His ideas helped shape a more dynamic, more practical view of psychology, focusing on how mental activities aid human adaptation and interaction with the world.

In summing up James's legacy, it's clear that his contributions extended far beyond his amusing name. He was a pivotal figure in the journey of psychology from a fledgling field to a central pillar of academic study in America. His focus on the purpose and utility of mental processes opened new doors in understanding the human mind, leaving a lasting impact on the field.

Psychoanalytic Theory

Dr. Sigmund Freud, MD (1890s)

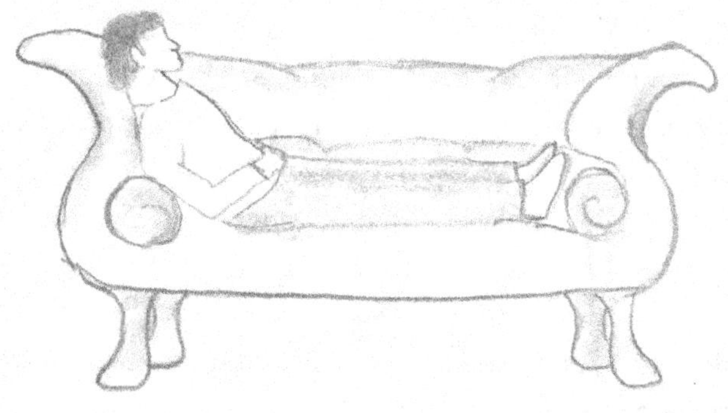

Front

Psychoanalytic Theory Definition: Human behavior and personality shaped by unconscious forces, drives, and childhood experiences.

Structures of Psyche:

1 Id: Instinctual drives.

2 Ego: Reality-oriented mediator.

3 Superego: Moral conscience.

Defense Mechanisms: Unconscious strategies to manage conflicts (repression, denial, projection, sublimation).

Childhood Experiences: Formative impact on adult personality and behavior.

Dream Analysis: Dreams as symbolic wish fulfillment and access to the unconscious.

Free Association: Technique revealing unconscious thoughts in therapy.

Back

Critiques: Lacks empirical evidence; subjective.

Overemphasis on sexual, aggressive drives.

Uncertain scientific validity.

Freud's Contributions:Explored unconscious, childhood influences.

Introduced dream analysis, defense mechanisms.

Pioneered talk therapy (free association).

Legacy: Influential despite controversies.

Inspired art, literature, and cultural understanding.

Complex relationship with Carl Jung; diverging theories.

Freud's Life: Controversial personal habits (cocaine use, cigar smoking).

Illness and assisted suicide.

Fascination with antiquities, religion, civilization.

Simple Definition of Psychoanalytic Theory

Psychoanalytic theory, introduced by Freud, posits that human behavior and personality are profoundly influenced by unconscious forces, drives, and childhood experiences.

More Detailed Explanation

Psychoanalytic theory, developed by Sigmund Freud in the late 1890s, revolutionized the understanding of human psychology. It contends that our actions and personality traits are largely shaped by unconscious processes, including repressed feelings, early childhood experiences, and primitive impulses (Freud, 1923). Freud argued that the unconscious mind is a reservoir of feelings, thoughts, and memories that are outside of conscious awareness, yet still significantly influence behavior.

A key component of this theory is the structural model of the psyche, which Freud divided into three parts: the id (instinctual drives), the ego (reality-oriented mediator), and the superego (moral conscience). The interactions and conflicts among these structures shape an individual's behavior and psychological state (Freud, 1923).

Freud also introduced the concept of defense mechanisms, unconscious psychological strategies employed to cope with reality and maintain self-image. Common defense mechanisms include repression, denial, projection, and sublimation (Freud,

1894).

General Critiques

Psychoanalytic theory has been widely critiqued for its lack of scientific rigor and reliance on unverifiable concepts. Critics argue that many of Freud's theories, particularly those related to sexual development and the Oedipus complex, are not empirically testable and are based on anecdotal evidence rather than scientific research (Popper, 1963).

Additionally, some argue that Freud's emphasis on sexual and aggressive drives as the primary motivators of human behavior is overly reductionist and ignores the complexity of human motivations (Grünbaum, 1984). Despite these critiques, psychoanalytic theory has had a lasting impact on psychology, contributing to our understanding of personality development, mental disorders, and therapeutic techniques.

Other Freudian Concepts:

Simple Definition of Childhood Experiences and Adult Behavior

The concept that childhood experiences significantly impact adult behavior suggests that the emotional and psychological experiences we undergo in early life play a crucial role in shaping our adult personality, behaviors, and emotional responses.

More Detailed Explanation

Freud's perspective on the influence of childhood experiences on adult behavior is a cornerstone of his psychoanalytic theory. He posited that the formative years are critical in shaping an individual's adult personality and psychological state (Freud, 1905). According to Freud, early experiences, especially those involving primary caregivers, leave an indelible mark on our emotional development.

A central aspect of this theory is Freud's psychosexual development stages, where he proposed that psychological conflicts experienced at specific stages could lead to characteristic adult behaviors or neuroses (Freud, 1905). For instance, the Oedipus complex, a concept developed by Freud, describes a stage where a child subconsciously experiences a sexual attraction towards the opposite-sex parent and rivalry towards the same-sex parent. If unresolved, these feelings could influence adult relationship dynamics (Freud, 1899).

Freud also introduced the concept of defense mechanisms, such as repression, which he believed were strategies developed in childhood to cope with emotional conflicts and stressors. These mechanisms, formed in response to early experiences, continue to influence behavior in adulthood (Freud, 1894).

General Critiques

While Freud's theories on the impact of childhood experiences on adult behavior have been highly influential, they have also faced criticism. Critics argue that Freud's theories often lack empirical evidence and rely too heavily on retrospective accounts, which can be subjective and unreliable (Jones,

1953). Additionally, some modern psychologists have critiqued Freud's emphasis on sexual and aggressive impulses in childhood development as overly deterministic and reflective of the cultural context of his time, rather than universal psychological principles (Kramer, 2006).

Dreams

Simple Definition of Dream Analysis

Dream analysis, according to Freud, is the practice of interpreting the content of dreams to uncover underlying thoughts and desires hidden in the unconscious mind.

More Detailed Explanation

Freud's dream analysis is a significant aspect of his psychoanalytic theory, where he posited that dreams are a form of wish fulfillment and provide a pathway to understanding the unconscious mind (Freud, 1900). He believed that the manifest content of a dream, or what we remember upon waking, is a symbolic representation of latent content – the unconscious wishes and desires.

For example, Freud suggested that a dream about flying could symbolize a latent desire for freedom or an escape from life's responsibilities. In this context, the act of flying represents an unfulfilled wish for liberation from constraints or a longing to rise above one's current situation (Freud, 1900).

Freud also explored the concept of dream symbols, arguing

that certain objects and scenarios in dreams are universally symbolic of specific themes or desires. He maintained that through the analysis of these symbols, one could access the hidden emotional and psychological states of the dreamer (Freud, 1917).

Critiques

Freud's dream analysis has been subject to various criticisms. One of the primary critiques is that his interpretations of dreams were often speculative and not empirically verifiable. Critics argue that the subjective nature of dream interpretation makes it difficult to establish objective or scientific conclusions about the unconscious mind (Grünbaum, 1984).

Additionally, some modern psychologists and researchers have questioned the universality of dream symbols proposed by Freud. They suggest that dream interpretations may be more influenced by individual experiences and cultural backgrounds than Freud's theory accounts for (Hobson, 2000).

Defense Mechanisms

(The List)

1. Repression: An unconscious mechanism employed by the ego to keep disturbing or threatening thoughts from becoming conscious (Freud, 1915).

1. Denial: The refusal to accept reality or fact, acting as if a painful event, thought, or feeling did not exist. It is a defense mechanism employed to avoid the discomfort of acknowledging an uncomfortable truth (Freud, 1923).

1. Projection: The misattribution of a person's undesired thoughts, feelings, or impulses onto another person who does not have those thoughts, feelings, or impulses. Projection is used especially when the thoughts are considered unacceptable for the person to express or they feel completely ill at ease with having them (Freud, 1894).

1. Displacement: The redirection of an impulse (usually aggression) onto a powerless substitute target. The target can be a person or an object that can serve as a symbolic substitute (Freud, 1894).

1. Sublimation: A defense mechanism that allows us to act out unacceptable impulses by converting these behaviors into a more acceptable form. For example, sublimating aggressive impulses by participating in competitive sports (Freud, 1905).

1. Reaction Formation: The converting of unwanted or dangerous thoughts, feelings, or impulses into their opposites. For instance, a person experiencing anger might display exaggerated friendliness (Freud, 1894).

1. Regression: A return to an earlier stage of development in the face of unacceptable thoughts or impulses. For example, an adult dealing with stress might begin to suck their thumb or throw temper tantrums (Freud, 1917).

1. Rationalization: Offering a socially acceptable and apparently more or less logical explanation for an act or decision actually produced by unconscious impulses. This is a defense mechanism that involves justifying behaviors or feelings in a rational or logical manner, avoiding the true reasons for the behavior (Freud, 1917).

1. Intellectualization: A defense mechanism where reasoning is used to block confrontation with an unconscious conflict and its associated emotional stress, by using intellectual processes (Freud, 1917).

1. Identification: An unconscious attempt to increase one's

self-esteem by adopting certain attributes and characteristics of an individual one admires (Freud, 1921).

2. Simple Definition of Defense Mechanisms

1. Defense mechanisms, as defined by Freud, are unconscious strategies that the mind employs to protect itself from anxiety and to cope with reality. These mechanisms can shield individuals from painful memories or uncomfortable truths.

More Detailed Explanation

Freud's concept of defense mechanisms involves various psychological strategies that individuals unconsciously use to protect themselves from anxieties stemming from unacceptable thoughts or feelings. He believed that these mechanisms operate at an unconscious level and help the ego to manage conflicts between the id and the superego (Freud, 1894).

For example, repression, one of the most fundamental defense mechanisms, involves unconsciously blocking out painful or uncomfortable memories or feelings. This mechanism acts as a psychological barrier, preventing distressing thoughts from entering conscious awareness. In the context of trauma, an individual might repress memories of the traumatic event as a way to avoid the pain associated with these memories (Freud, 1915).

Another example is denial, where an individual refuses to accept reality or facts, thereby protecting themselves from facing uncomfortable truths or emotions associated with those facts. For instance, someone might deny the severity of a personal problem, such as addiction, as a way to avoid confronting the negative implications of the issue (Freud, 1923).

General Critiques

While Freud's theory of defense mechanisms has been influential in understanding human psychology, it has faced criticism for its lack of empirical evidence and its reliance on unobservable psychological processes. Critics argue that because these mechanisms operate unconsciously, they are difficult to measure or objectively study (Popper, 1963).

Furthermore, some contemporary psychologists have argued that Freud's emphasis on defense mechanisms as primarily protective and unconscious may oversimplify the complex nature of how individuals cope with stress and trauma. Modern psychology tends to view coping strategies on a broader spectrum, including conscious and adaptive mechanisms (Vaillant, 1977).

Free Association (talk therapy)

Simple Definition of Free Association

Free association is a therapeutic technique where a person speaks freely about whatever comes to mind, allowing unconscious thoughts and feelings to be expressed and explored.

More Detailed Explanation

Free association, a cornerstone in Freudian psychoanalysis, is a method wherein the patient is encouraged to verbalize thoughts, feelings, and images as they occur, without censorship or filtering. This process is intended to tap into the unconscious part of the mind, revealing the hidden meanings and motivations behind thoughts and behaviors (Freud, 1895).

Freud believed that in normal conversation, the conscious mind acts as a censor, controlling and suppressing the deeper thoughts and feelings of the unconscious mind. Free association bypasses this censorship, allowing the therapist to explore the deeper layers of the psyche. This method can reveal the underlying, often repressed, conflicts and emotions that contribute to psychological distress.

For example, a patient may start talking about a recent event and, through free association, eventually uncover deeper feelings connected to past experiences. This technique is also used to explore dreams, where the patient recounts their dream and then freely associates to various elements of the dream, uncovering the latent content behind the manifest content of the dream (Freud, 1900).

General Critiques

While free association has been fundamental in psychoanalytic therapy, it has its critiques. Some critics argue that the technique lacks structure and can lead to interpretative biases by the therapist. Without more structured guidance, there is a risk that the therapist might impose interpretations that are not reflective of the patient's true thoughts and feelings (Grünbaum, 1984).

Moreover, the effectiveness of free association as a therapeutic tool has been questioned, with some suggesting that it might not be as effective in addressing certain psychological conditions as more structured, evidence-based therapies (Kramer, 2006).

Biography of Sigmund Freud

Sigmund Freud, oh, where to start with this character? Here's a man who was as enigmatic as the theories he propounded. Known for his love affair with cocaine, which he didn't just dabble in but embraced wholeheartedly, Freud was a figure who was constantly churning out ideas and theories, some of which were as controversial as his lifestyle.

Freud was the architect of the psychoanalytic model, a framework that delved deep into the recesses of the human mind, unraveling the complexities of the id, ego, and superego. He pioneered the technique of free association, laying the groundwork for what we now know as talk therapy (Freud, 1895). His interpretations of dreams were not just an analysis but a full exploration into what he believed was the window to the unconscious (Freud, 1900).

The man was a chain-smoker of cigars, a habit that eventually led to a grim battle with jaw cancer, culminating in his assisted suicide—a decision that perhaps reflected his lifelong confrontation with the darker aspects of human existence (Jones,

1953). Freud's personal life and his professional inquiries were deeply intertwined, each feeding into and informing the other.

Criticism of Freud has been as relentless as his theories were groundbreaking. When you're that high on cocaine, working out the kinks of human psychology, particularly in the context of women's unconscious minds, it's almost a given that some personal biases might slip through. But here's the thing: despite the controversies and the criticisms, Freud's contributions to psychology are undeniable. His insights into the unconscious mind, the development of talk therapy, and the exploration of childhood experiences in shaping adult behavior have had a lasting impact on the field.

I'll admit, my view of Freud has evolved. I used to be more critical, seeing him as a man grasping at psychological straws. But over time, I've come to appreciate the complexity of his work. Yes, some of his theories seem almost obvious now, but back then, they were revolutionary. The fact that he could uncover these 'obvious' truths when no one else had is, in itself, impressive.

In sum, Freud's life was a tapestry of brilliance, controversy, and paradoxes. He was a man deeply embroiled in his theories, a product of his time, yet ahead of it in many ways. His legacy in psychology isn't just about the specific theories he proposed but about the broader understanding of the human mind and behavior that he helped pioneer.

Freud MISC: Exploring the Lesser-Known Aspects of Freud's Work

Freud's Views on Religion and Civilization

Freud had quite a bit to say about religion and culture. In his book "The Future of an Illusion" (1927), Freud considered religion as a collective neurosis. He argued that religious beliefs were illusions, fulfillments of the oldest, strongest, and most urgent wishes of mankind (Freud, 1927). Then, in "Civilization and Its Discontents" (1930), he talked about the tension between individual's quest for freedom and civilization's demand for conformity and instinctual repression. He saw civilization as a way to curb destructive human desires, but at the cost of individual happiness (Freud, 1930).

Freud's Fascination with Antiquities

Did you know Freud was an avid collector of antiquities? His office and home were littered with ancient statues and artifacts. Freud believed these objects held symbolic meanings and provided a connection to the past. His collection was not just a hobby; it was a reflection of his deep interest in history, archaeology, and the human psyche (Gay, 1988).

Freud's Relationship with Carl Jung

Freud's relationship with Carl Jung was complex and fraught with intellectual tension. Initially, Jung was seen as a protégé of Freud. However, as Jung's ideas began to diverge, particularly with his concept of the collective unconscious, their relationship became strained. The split between Freud and Jung was significant, marking a major fork in the road for psychoanalytic theory (Kerr, 1994).

Freud's Concept of 'Death Drive'

Apart from his theories on sex and aggression, Freud also

introduced the concept of the 'death drive' (Thanatos), which he proposed in "Beyond the Pleasure Principle" (1920). This controversial idea suggested that humans hold an unconscious desire to die or return to a state of inactivity, opposing the life instincts (Eros) (Freud, 1920).

Freud's Influence on Art and Literature

Freud's influence extended beyond the realm of psychology into art and literature. His exploration of the unconscious inspired many artists and writers to delve deeper into the human psyche. Surrealists, in particular, were influenced by Freud's ideas, as they sought to explore the unconscious mind in their artworks (Gay, 1988).

Behaviorism

Dr. John B. Watson, PhD (1913)

Front:

Concept: Behaviorism

Focus: Observable behaviors shaped by environmental interactions

Pioneer: John B. Watson (1913)

Core Principles: Emphasizes conditioning as a primary mechanism for learning.

Advocates for a scientific approach based on observable outcomes.

Back:

Applications: Classical Conditioning: Demonstrated with the Little Albert experiment.

Behavior Modification: Applied in therapy, education, and parenting.

Critiques: Criticized for neglecting internal mental states and cognitive processes.

Legacy: Watson's work laid the groundwork for behavior analysis and modern behavior modification techniques, influencing both psychology and marketing.

Simple Definition of Behaviorism

Behaviorism is a theory in psychology that focuses on observable behaviors, arguing that all behaviors are learned through interaction with the environment, rather than innate or inherited traits.

More Detailed Explanation

Developed by John B. Watson in 1913, behaviorism marked a

significant shift in the focus of psychological research. Watson posited that psychology should be a science based on observable behavior, not on the internal mental state or consciousness. According to behaviorism, all behaviors are the result of conditioning and can be altered through changes in the environment (Watson, 1913).

A key aspect of behaviorism is the concept of stimulus-response. Watson and later behaviorists argued that behavior could be understood and predicted based on the stimuli present in the environment and the organism's history of interaction with these stimuli.

Real-World Examples of Behaviorism

Little Albert experiment in 1920.

Classical Conditioning: The concept of classical conditioning emerged as a key aspect of behaviorism, illustrated vividly by John B. Watson's famous Little Albert experiment in 1920. This experiment demonstrated that it was possible to condition an emotional reaction in a human being, specifically a child, through controlled environmental stimuli (Watson & Rayner, 1920).

In the Little Albert experiment, Watson and his assistant Rosalie Rayner exposed a young child, Albert, to a series of stimuli. Initially, Albert showed no fear of a white rat. However, Watson and Rayner then paired the presence of the rat with a loud, frightening noise. After repeated pairings, Albert began to show signs of fear when presented with the rat, even in the absence of the noise. This response indicated that a conditioned emotional reaction (fear of the rat) had been successfully established.

This experiment is a classic example of classical conditioning, where a neutral stimulus (the white rat) becomes associated with an unconditioned stimulus (the loud noise) that naturally elicits an unconditioned response (fear). After repeated pairings, the neutral stimulus alone starts to evoke a conditioned response (fear), indicating that learning has occurred.

Operant Conditioning: B.F. Skinner, a behaviorist, showed that behaviors could be shaped by rewards or punishments. For instance, rewarding a child with praise for completing homework can reinforce the behavior of doing homework.

Behavior Modification

Behavior Modification: Behavior modification, rooted in the principles of behaviorism, is a therapeutic approach used to change undesirable behaviors by employing techniques based on the theories of classical and operant conditioning. This approach is often used in various therapeutic settings, including the treatment of phobias, behavioral disorders, and other psychological problems.

In behavior modification, the focus is on changing behaviors through different reinforcement strategies and conditioning techniques. One common method is exposure therapy, especially effective in treating phobias.

Exposure Therapy in Treating Phobias

Exposure therapy is a process where individuals are gradually and systematically exposed to the object or situation they fear. The underlying principle is to desensitize the individual to the fear stimulus and reduce the conditioned response (fear) associated with it. This method aligns with the principles of classical conditioning by gradually reducing the learned association between the feared object and the anxiety response.

For example, in treating arachnophobia (fear of spiders), a person might first be asked to think about spiders, then look at pictures of spiders, and eventually progress to being in the same room with a spider. Over time and through repeated exposure, the anxiety response diminishes, eventually allowing the individual to confront the feared object without significant distress.

Behavior Modification in Other Areas

1. Behavioral Disorders in Children: Techniques like positive reinforcement and time-outs are used to encourage desirable behaviors and discourage unwanted behaviors in children.
2. Addiction Treatment: Behavior modification is employed in addiction treatment programs, where positive behaviors (e.g., attending therapy sessions) are reinforced, while strategies are developed to reduce the addictive behavior.
3. Weight Loss and Healthy Habits: Behavior modification strategies are used to encourage healthy eating and exercise habits. Reinforcements and rewards are employed to encourage the desired behaviors.

Critiques of Behavior Modification

While behavior modification has been effective in various therapeutic contexts, it has faced criticisms. Some argue that this approach can be overly simplistic, focusing solely on observable behaviors without considering underlying psychological factors or cognitive processes (Skinner, 1953). Additionally, ethical concerns arise when behavior modification involves control or manipulation of behavior without considering the individual's autonomy and well-being.

Education and Learning in Behaviorism

Education and Learning: Behaviorism's impact on education is profound, particularly in the methods used to structure learning environments and manage classroom behavior. The theory's emphasis on reinforcement has reshaped educational approaches, focusing on promoting learning and discipline through behavior modification.

Reinforcement in Education

Reinforcement in educational settings serves to strengthen desirable behaviors such as active participation, timely assignment completion, and adherence to classroom rules.

Positive Reinforcement: This involves offering rewards or positive outcomes following desirable behaviors. In a classroom setting, positive reinforcement might include verbal praise, extra playtime, or tangible rewards like stickers for good behavior or high academic performance. This approach encourages students to repeat the positive behavior to receive similar rewards in the future (Skinner, 1953).

Negative Reinforcement: Contrary to its name, negative reinforcement involves removing an unpleasant stimulus in response to a positive behavior. For instance, a teacher might reduce homework for the entire class if they maintain good discipline or perform well in a test. This method encourages students to exhibit the desired behavior to avoid something they don't like (Skinner, 1953).

Behavioral Shaping: Teachers often use this technique to gradually guide students towards a desired behavior by reinforcing successive approximations of the target behavior. For example, initially rewarding a child for sitting at their desk for a short period, and gradually increasing the time requirement for the reward (Skinner, 1957).

Token Economies: This involves giving tokens for good behavior or performance, which can later be exchanged for a reward. This system helps in instilling discipline and motivation in the classroom (Kazdin, 1982).

Critiques of Behaviorism in Education

While behaviorism has been influential in education, it has also faced criticisms. Critics argue that this approach may overlook intrinsic motivation – learning for the sake of learning rather than for external rewards. Others point out that an over-reliance on rewards might diminish a student's natural interest in a subject (Deci, 1971).

Moreover, behaviorism's focus on observable behavior may not fully address the complexities of the learning process, such as cognitive and emotional factors (Bandura, 1977).

Critiques of Behaviorism

Behaviorism has been criticized for its oversimplification of human behavior and for ignoring mental processes. Critics argue that behaviorism overlooks the importance of cognitive processes, emotions, and internal states in understanding behavior. Additionally, the ethical implications of experiments like the Little Albert study have been questioned (Chomsky, 1959).

Biography of John B. Watson

John B. Watson, now there's a name that stirs up some mixed feelings. On the one hand, you've got to give it to the guy for his scientific ingenuity. His work in psychology, notably the Little Albert experiment, was, to put it mildly, ethically iffy, but it undeniably paved the way for behaviorism. His approach was hands-on and results-driven, something I've always seen as the bread and butter of real psychological science. It reminds me of the good old days of my doctoral studies, where results and practical applications were the name of the game.

But Watson was more than just a psychologist; he was a man of complexities and contradictions. After his stint in academia, he jumped ship to the world of advertising. Here, he applied his understanding of human behavior to influence consumer habits. The guy was a natural; he knew what made people tick and wasn't shy about using that knowledge to sell products. His transition into advertising could be seen as pioneering, laying the foundation for many of the marketing tactics we see today (Buckley, 1989).

However, I always catch myself when I start to admire Watson too much. Let's not sugarcoat it – some of his methods in psychology were questionable, and his foray into advertising was a bit like using science to manipulate the masses. It's a bit ironic, really. Here was a man who could dissect human behavior to its most basic elements, yet his legacy in advertising somewhat contributed to the complex, often manipulative consumer culture we find ourselves in today.

In summing up Watson, I see him as a bit of a double-edged sword. Brilliant? Undoubtedly. Controversial? Absolutely. His scientific work was groundbreaking, but it's hard to ignore the ethical shadows it cast. And his influence on advertising – well, it's like he opened Pandora's box, showing the world how to tap into the psyche for profit. In a way, Watson's story is a reminder of the fine line between understanding human behavior and exploiting it.

Classical Conditioning

Dr. Ivan Pavlov, MD (1890s)

Front:

Simple Definition: Learning where a natural stimulus pairs with a neutral one to trigger a learned response.

Pavlov's Discovery (1890s): Noticed dogs salivating at bells paired with food, illustrating conditioned responses.

Key Concepts Stimuli Pairing: Natural (unconditioned) and neutral stimuli combined to produce a conditioned response.

Applications: Fear responses in humans, advertising strategies (product associations).

Real-World Examples

Fear Conditioning: Neutral stimulus (e.g., thunder) linked with trauma activates fear.

Advertising: Products paired with positive stimuli (music, celebrities) to evoke desired emotions.

Back:

Treatments, Critiques, and Pavlov's Ethical Considerations

Treatment Techniques Systematic Desensitization: Gradual exposure to fear stimuli with relaxation techniques.

Exposure Therapy: Controlled exposure to diminish fear responses.

Critiques

Behavior Oversimplification: Ignores cognitive processes and complex behaviors.

Ethical Concerns: Animal research ethics, particularly Pavlov's methods.

Pavlov's Legacy Foundational in psychology despite ethical debates.

Highlighted the importance of stimulus-response learning, with broad applications from clinical psychology to marketing.

Simple Definition of Classical Conditioning

Classical conditioning is a learning process where a naturally occurring stimulus is paired with a previously neutral stimulus to elicit a conditioned response (Pavlov, 1927).

Expanded Definition of Classical Conditioning

Developed by Ivan Pavlov in the 1890s, classical conditioning is a fundamental theory in psychology that demonstrates how certain stimuli can be used to trigger a conditioned response (Pavlov, 1927). Originally studying digestion in dogs, Pavlov discovered that stimuli, when paired with an unconditioned stimulus, could produce a learned, or conditioned, response. The most notable example is the Pavlovian response, where dogs were conditioned to salivate at the sound of a bell, previously associated only with food.

Real-World Examples of Classical Conditioning

Fear Conditioning in Humans: Mechanism of Fear Conditioning: During a traumatic event, the amygdala, a key part of the brain's limbic system, becomes highly active. This region of the brain is crucial for processing emotions, especially fear. When a neutral stimulus (such as thunder) coincides with a frightening experience (like a traumatic storm), the amygdala associates the two. Later, the sound of thunder alone can activate the amygdala, triggering a fear response (LeDoux, 1996).

Generalization of Fear: Over time, this fear response can generalize beyond the specific stimulus. For example, someone who develops a fear of thunder may also start to feel anxious with other loud noises or even with dark clouds that suggest the possibility of a storm. This generalization can make the fear more pervasive and challenging to manage (Dunsmoor et al., 2015).

Long-Term Impact: Fear conditioning can have long-term effects on a person's behavior and emotional state. It can lead to avoidance behaviors, where the person goes out of their way to avoid the feared stimulus, significantly impacting their daily life and potentially leading to conditions like phobias or generalized anxiety disorder (Craske et al., 2009).

Treatment and Desensitization: Understanding the process of fear conditioning is essential for treating phobias and anxiety disorders. Techniques like systematic desensitization or exposure therapy are often used to gradually reduce the fear response. This treatment involves controlled exposure to the feared stimulus in a safe environment, allowing the person to experience the stimulus without the feared outcome, thereby weakening the conditioned fear response (Wolpe, 1958).

Advertising: advertising, classical conditioning is employed to create associations between products and desirable stimuli. The aim is to condition consumers to have positive feelings about a product by pairing it with stimuli that already evoke positive emotions. For example, a car commercial might pair images of the vehicle with picturesque landscapes and soothing music, intending to transfer the feelings evoked by these sights and sounds to the car itself (Gorn, 1982).

Examples and In-Depth Analysis

Pairing with Popular Music: Advertisers often use popular or catchy music in commercials. The positive feelings elicited by the music can become associated with the product being advertised. Over time, just seeing the product may evoke the same positive emotions that the music does (Gorn, 1982).

Celebrity Endorsements: When a product is endorsed by a celebrity, consumers may associate the positive qualities of the celebrity (like attractiveness or success) with the product. This association is a form of classical conditioning where the celebrity (unconditioned stimulus) is paired with the product (neutral stimulus), and the positive perception of the celebrity becomes associated with the product (Keller, 1987).

Emotional Appeal in Commercials: Advertisements that create emotional narratives, especially those that evoke happiness, nostalgia, or even sadness, can lead to a conditioned emotional response to the product. When consumers later encounter the product, they may recall the emotional response elicited by the advertisement (Bagozzi, Gopinath, & Nyer, 1999).

Use of Colors and Visuals: The strategic use of colors and visuals in advertisements can also condition consumer responses. For example, the color red can evoke excitement and energy and is often used in ads to create these associations with the product (Bellizzi & Hite, 1992).

Phobias and Treatment:Phobias, which are intense, irrational fears of specific objects or situations, can often be traced back to a conditioning process. This is where a neutral stimulus (e.g., a spider) becomes associated with a frightening experience, leading to a conditioned fear response whenever the stimulus is encountered (Öhman & Mineka, 2001). For instance, if someone has a panic attack in an elevator, they might develop a phobia of elevators, associating them with feelings of fear and panic, even though elevators themselves are not inherently dangerous.

Treatment of Phobias: Counterconditioning and Exposure Therapy

Systematic Desensitization: This therapy, developed by Joseph Wolpe, involves gradually exposing the patient to the fear stimulus in a controlled and supportive environment. The process starts with learning relaxation techniques, then gradually confronting the feared object or situation in a hierarchical manner, starting from the least to the most anxiety-provoking scenarios (Wolpe, 1958). For example, someone with a fear of flying might first be asked to think about flying, then watch videos of planes, and eventually work up to taking an actual flight.

Flooding: Unlike systematic desensitization, flooding involves immediate and intense exposure to the fear stimulus. This approach is based on the idea that fear responses have a natural tendency to diminish over time as the individual learns that the fear stimulus is not harmful (Marks, 1987).

Virtual Reality Exposure: This modern approach uses virtual reality technology to expose individuals to their fear stimuli in a safe, controlled environment. It's particularly useful for phobias where real-world exposure is impractical or too intense at the initial stages of therapy (Rothbaum et al., 1995).

Cognitive Behavioral Therapy (CBT): CBT helps patients understand the thoughts and feelings that influence behaviors. It is often used in conjunction with exposure therapy, helping individuals to challenge and change their irrational fears and beliefs about the feared object or situation (Clark, 2013).

Critiques and Considerations

While these treatments are generally effective, they're not without their critiques. Some individuals may find exposure therapies too distressing, potentially leading to dropout or worsening of symptoms if not carefully managed (Choy et al., 2007). Furthermore, treatments need to be personalized, as phobias are often intertwined with individual histories and psychological profiles.

In sum, understanding and treating phobias through the lens of classical conditioning not only demystifies these intense fears but also provides a structured approach to overcoming them, blending both psychological understanding and therapeutic intervention.

Critiques of Classical Conditioning

Oversimplification of Human Behavior: One of the primary critiques of classical conditioning is its reductionist approach to human behavior. Critics argue that it oversimplifies complex human behaviors and emotions by reducing them to simple stimulus-response mechanisms. This viewpoint suggests that classical conditioning does not adequately account for the myriad of factors influencing human behavior, such as cognitive processes, cultural influences, and personal experiences (Brewer, 1974).

Neglect of Cognitive Processes: Critics have pointed out that classical conditioning largely ignores the role of cognitive processes in learning. It overlooks how individuals' thoughts, beliefs, and expectations can influence their responses to stimuli. This critique is particularly relevant in the context of treating phobias and anxiety, where cognitive factors play a significant role (Bouton, Mineka, & Barlow, 2001).

Ethical Concerns in Research: The ethical implications of some classical conditioning experiments, particularly those involving animals, have raised concerns. Critics argue that some of the methods used in classical conditioning research, such as those in Pavlov's experiments, can be considered inhumane or cruel. This critique extends to the general use of animals in psychological research, questioning the morality of using animals to understand human psychology (Rollin, 1989).

Limited Scope in Explaining Complex Behaviors: While classical conditioning explains certain types of learning, it does not encompass the breadth of human learning and behavior. Complex behaviors, especially those involving higher cognitive functions, are often beyond the scope of what classical conditioning can explain. This limitation has led to the development of other theories, such as operant conditioning and social learning theory, which attempt to fill in the gaps left by classical conditioning (Skinner, 1950).

Biography

Pavlov, hailed for his contribution to psychology, was, at his core, a physiologist. His journey into the realms of what we now know as classical conditioning wasn't driven by a quest to understand the human psyche but rather a byproduct of his physiological research (Todes, 2002). It's ironic, really, how someone not initially aiming to delve into psychology ended up being such a pivotal figure in the field.

But let's not beat around the bush. Pavlov's methods with his dogs, the very crux of his experiments, were, by today's standards, far from ethical. The popular imagery of dogs drooling into a bowl at the sound of a bell is a cleaned-up version of a much grimmer reality. Pavlov's experiments involved invasive surgeries on the dogs to collect and measure saliva, a process that, frankly, veers into the territory of animal cruelty (Windholz, 1997). It's unsettling, to say the least.

His approach to research, a reflection of the scientific norms of his era, serves as a stark example of how the pursuit of knowledge sometimes overshadowed ethical considerations, especially in animal research. This aspect of Pavlov's legacy is a jarring reminder of the ethical evolution in scientific research. While we can't deny the importance of his findings in behavioral psychology, it's imperative to view his work through a lens that acknowledges the ethical shortcomings (Birke, 2002).

Pavlov's story is a bit of a cautionary tale, emblematic of the 'Great Man' narrative that often glosses over the more problematic aspects of scientific pioneers. His contributions to psychology were significant, no doubt, but they came at a cost that today would be deemed unacceptable. It's a complex legacy, one that invites us to ponder the ethical dimensions and historical context of scientific exploration (Hearst, 1991).

Operant Conditioning

Dr. B.F. Skinner, PhD (1930s)

Front:

Concept: Operant Conditioning

Focus: Learning through consequences (rewards/punishments)

Pioneer: B.F. Skinner (1930s)

Core Principles:Behaviors followed by positive outcomes are likely to recur.

Behaviors followed by negative outcomes are less likely to recur.

Back:

Applications:Education: Positive reinforcement to enhance student motivation.

Workplace: Negative reinforcement to improve productivity.

Parenting: Punishment to decrease undesirable behaviors.

Therapy: Behavior modification for treating disorders.

Critiques:Viewed as mechanistic; may overlook emotional and cognitive aspects.

Legacy:Foundation for behavior analysis and modification techniques.

Simple Definition of Operant Conditioning

Operant conditioning is a learning process where behavior is shaped and maintained by its consequences, such as rewards or punishments (Skinner, 1938).

Expanded Definition of Operant Conditioning

Pioneered by B.F. Skinner in the 1930s, operant conditioning is a cornerstone of behavioral psychology, focusing on how consequences influence the likelihood of a behavior's recurrence. Skinner's theory posits that behaviors followed by positive outcomes tend to be repeated, while those followed by negative outcomes are less likely to be repeated. Unlike classical conditioning, which involves involuntary responses, operant conditioning deals with voluntary behaviors (Skinner, 1953).

Real-World Examples of Operant Conditioning

Positive Reinforcement in Education:Implementation in the Classroom:
Positive reinforcement in educational settings involves acknowledging and rewarding desired behaviors to encourage their recurrence. When teachers praise students for good work, offer stickers for completed assignments, or provide extra playtime for positive classroom behavior, they are using positive reinforcement. These rewards make it more likely that the students will repeat the good behavior in the future (Skinner, 1953).

Impact on Student Motivation: By recognizing and rewarding positive behaviors, teachers can significantly boost students' motivation. Positive reinforcement can help students develop a connection between effort and success, fostering a more engaging and productive learning environment (Kazdin, 1982).

Customizing Reinforcement: Effective use of positive reinforcement requires understanding what motivates individual students. While some may respond well to verbal praise, others might find tangible rewards or privileges more motivating. This personalization ensures that the reinforcement is meaningful and effective for each student (Deci, 1971).

Long-Term Educational Benefits: Consistent positive reinforcement can help in shaping students' long-term academic behaviors. For instance, students who receive regular positive feedback for timely homework submission are likely to develop strong study habits and time management skills, which are beneficial throughout their educational journey (Maag, 2001).

Critiques and Considerations: While positive reinforcement can be highly effective, over-reliance on extrinsic rewards has been critiqued for potentially undermining intrinsic motivation. Some educators argue that the constant need for external rewards may diminish students' internal drive to learn for learning's sake (Ryan & Deci, 2000). Therefore, it's essential for educators to balance tangible rewards with strategies that foster intrinsic motivation, such as nurturing students' natural curiosity and promoting a love of learning.

Negative Reinforcement in the Workplace:Definition and Application:
Negative reinforcement in a workplace context involves the removal of an unpleasant or undesirable condition in response to a desired behavior. Contrary to common perception, negative reinforcement is not about punishing employees; rather, it's about encouraging desirable behaviors by taking away or avoiding negative workplace conditions (Skinner, 1953).

Examples in Work Settings: A common example is reducing

tedious tasks for an employee who meets or exceeds their targets. Here, the removal of an undesirable element (tedious tasks) acts as a reinforcement for productive behavior (meeting targets). Another instance could be allowing more flexible work hours for employees who consistently demonstrate high productivity. In this case, the removal of strict scheduling reinforces the behavior of maintaining high productivity levels (Kazdin, 1982).

Impact on Employee Motivation and Productivity: By removing obstacles or unpleasant aspects of a job, employers can enhance employee motivation and satisfaction. This form of reinforcement acknowledges that sometimes the best way to motivate employees is not just by adding rewards but by eliminating factors that may cause dissatisfaction or hinder performance (Maag, 2001).

Balancing with Positive Reinforcement: While negative reinforcement can be effective in certain contexts, it's crucial to balance it with positive reinforcement. Relying solely on negative reinforcement might create an environment where employees only work to avoid negative outcomes rather than to achieve positive ones, which could potentially harm morale and intrinsic motivation (Ryan & Deci, 2000).

Ethical and Practical Considerations: Employers need to be cautious in using negative reinforcement. Its misuse can lead to a stressful atmosphere where employees feel they are working under constant threat of negative consequences. Therefore, it should be applied thoughtfully and ethically, ensuring that it aligns with overall positive workplace culture and employee well-being (Deci, 1971).

Punishment in Parenting:

Definition and Implementation: In operant conditioning, punishment refers to a consequence that decreases the likelihood of a behavior being repeated. In the context of parenting, this can involve implementing a negative consequence (like a time-out) or taking away a privilege (like screen time) in response to undesirable behavior. This method is intended to teach children that certain behaviors are unacceptable (Skinner, 1953).

Examples and Practical Application: Common forms of punishment in parenting include time-outs, where a child is removed from an enjoyable environment or activity for a brief period. Another example is the loss of privileges, such as taking away a favorite toy or restricting playtime as a consequence of misbehavior. These actions are intended to provide immediate feedback that the behavior is unacceptable and should be avoided in the future (Kazdin, 1982).

Balancing with Positive Reinforcement: While punishment can be effective in reducing unwanted behavior, it's important to balance it with positive reinforcement. Constantly focusing on punishing negative behaviors without acknowledging and rewarding positive behaviors can lead to a negative atmosphere in the home. Children should understand what behaviors are expected of them, not just what behaviors to avoid (Ryan & Deci, 2000).

Considerations for Effective Use: For punishment to be effective, it must be consistent, immediately following the undesirable behavior, and proportionate to the behavior. Parents need to ensure that the punishment is not overly harsh and is appropriate for the child's age and understanding. It's also crucial for parents to explain why the behavior is unacceptable and what can be done differently in the future (Maag, 2001).

Potential Negative Effects: Over-reliance on punishment or excessively harsh punishments can have detrimental effects on children, including increased aggression, fear, anxiety, and damage to the parent-child relationship. Punishment should be used judiciously and always within the context of a loving and supportive relationship. Parents should strive to understand the reasons behind a child's behavior and address underlying issues, not just the behavior itself (Gershoff, 2002).

Behavior Modification in Therapy: Application and Techniques: Behavior modification in therapy involves the systematic application of operant conditioning principles to change maladaptive or harmful behaviors. This approach can include the use of positive reinforcement to encourage desirable behaviors, negative reinforcement to discourage undesirable behaviors, and punishment to reduce harmful behaviors. Common techniques include token economies, where individuals earn tokens for positive behaviors that can be exchanged for rewards, and contingency contracts, where the therapist and client agree on specific behavioral goals and rewards (Kazdin, 1982).

Treatment of Specific Disorders: Behavior modification has been effectively used in treating a variety of disorders, including ADHD, autism spectrum disorders, eating disorders, and substance abuse. For example, in treating ADHD, children may receive points or rewards for completing tasks or exhibiting self-control, which helps in reinforcing attention and focus (Pelham & Fabiano, 2008).

Use in Cognitive Behavioral Therapy (CBT): Behavior modification techniques are often integrated into CBT, a therapy that combines behavioral and cognitive approaches. In CBT, clients learn to identify and change maladaptive thought patterns while also working on changing behaviors that contribute to their problems (Beck, 1979).

Parent Training Programs: Behavior modification is also used in parent training programs to address behavioral issues in children. Parents learn to apply operant conditioning techniques, such as consistent reinforcement and appropriate discipline strategies, to improve their children's behavior (Webster-Stratton & Reid, 2003).

Challenges and Considerations: While behavior modification can be effective, it's important to consider individual differences in responsiveness to various reinforcement strategies. Therapists must be cautious not to over-rely on external rewards, as this can undermine intrinsic motivation. Additionally, ethical considerations must be taken into account, especially when using punishment as a form of behavior modification (Ryan & Deci, 2000).

In summary, behavior modification in therapy is a versatile and effective approach for addressing a wide range of behavioral and psychological issues. Its success relies on the careful application of operant conditioning principles, tailored to the individual needs and circumstances of each client, and balanced with a consideration of intrinsic motivation and ethical practice.

Critiques of Operant Conditioning

Operant conditioning has been critiqued for its mechanistic view of human behavior, suggesting it ignores the complexity of human emotions and cognitive processes (Chomsky, 1959). Critics argue that it oversimplifies the nuances of human behavior and does not fully account for intrinsic motivation or the influence of innate factors (Deci, 1971).

Biography of B.F. Skinner

B.F. Skinner, a towering figure in psychology, was a man whose ideas were as influential as they were contentious. Known primarily for his work on operant conditioning, Skinner was not just a psychologist; he was a provocateur in the scientific community. He stirred the pot with his views on human behavior, which some might say bordered on a deterministic view of human nature.

Skinner's work, particularly his experiments with the Skinner Box, where he studied the behavior of rats and pigeons, has been both lauded and criticized. The Skinner Box became a symbol of his approach to psychology – one that some have described as overly mechanical and reductionist (Bjork, 1993). He wasn't just shaping animal behaviors; he was shaping the very way we think about human behavior and learning.

But let's not gloss over the fact that Skinner's theories, while revolutionary, were also a bit divisive. His emphasis on behavior modification and control, especially in his utopian vision outlined in "Walden Two," raised eyebrows and ethical concerns. It wasn't just about understanding behavior; for Skinner, it was about controlling it, which, understandably, didn't sit well with everyone (Skinner, 1948).

In looking at Skinner's legacy, it's a mix of respect and caution. His contributions to behaviorism and educational methods are undeniable. Yet, his views often challenge our comfort zones, especially when it comes to notions of free will and autonomy. Skinner's story is a testament to the idea that in psychology, as in life, there are no simple answers – only complex, intriguing questions.

Analytical Psychology

Dr. Carl Jung, MD (1912)

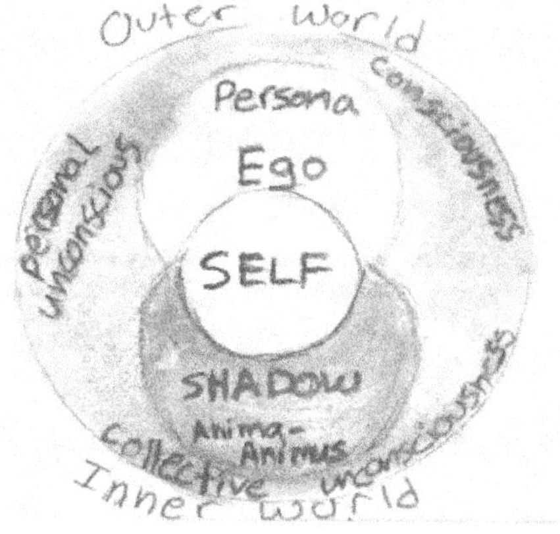
Outer world
Persona
Consciousness
Ego
Personal unconscious
SELF
SHADOW
Anima-
Animus
Collective unconsciousness
Inner world

Front:

Concept: Analytical Psychology

Pioneer: Carl Jung (1912)

Key Elements: Collective unconscious, archetypes, individuation.

Core Ideas:Explores the interplay between conscious and unconscious mind.

Introduces universal symbols across cultures, manifesting in dreams and myths.

Back:

Applications:Dream Analysis: A window into the unconscious.

Active Imagination: Engaging with and interpreting dream symbols.

Individuation: Integrating unconscious elements for personal growth.

Impact & Critiques:Significant in psychotherapy; criticized for subjective nature and empirical challenges.

Legacy:Offers a rich, symbolic framework for psychological exploration and healing.

Simple Definition of Analytical Psychology

Analytical psychology, pioneered by Carl Jung in 1912, is a branch of psychology that explores the deeper layers of the psyche through concepts such as the collective unconscious, archetypes, and individuation (Jung, 1912).

Expanded Definition of Analytical Psychology

Carl Jung's analytical psychology delves into the complex interplay between the conscious and unconscious parts of the mind. Unlike his contemporary Sigmund Freud, Jung introduced the idea of the collective unconscious—a shared part of the unconscious that contains memories and ideas inherited from our ancestors. This theory suggests that there are universal symbols and motifs, or archetypes, that emerge in dreams, myths, and art across cultures. Jung believed that the process of individuation, or the integration of these unconscious elements into consciousness, is crucial for psychological development and self-realization (Jung, 1959).

Real-World Examples of Analytical Psychology

Dream Analysis: Dream analysis is a central pillar in Carl Jung's approach to understanding the unconscious mind. Jung posited that dreams are a window into the unconscious, revealing both personal and collective unconscious content. Unlike Freud, who viewed dreams primarily as wish fulfillment, Jung saw them as meaningful expressions of unconscious processes, aimed at communicating with the conscious mind to achieve psychological balance (Jung, 1974).

The Role of Symbols: Jung emphasized the symbolic nature of dreams. He believed that dreams often use symbols to represent complex concepts that the conscious mind struggles to comprehend. These symbols, drawn from the collective unconscious, carry universal meanings across different cultures and historical periods, reflecting shared human experiences and archetypes (Jung, 1959).

Active Imagination Technique: Jung developed the active imagination technique as a way to engage with and interpret the symbols presented in dreams. This method involves the dreamer entering a meditative state to revisit their dream and interact with its components, allowing for a deeper exploration of its meaning and relevance to the individual's life (Jung, 1966).

Individuation Process: Dream analysis is integral to Jung's concept of individuation—the process of integrating unconscious elements into consciousness to achieve self-realization. By examining and understanding the symbols and motifs in their dreams, individuals can uncover insights about their psychological development and unresolved issues, facilitating personal growth (Jung, 1959).

Case Studies and Clinical Application: Jung often used dream analysis in his clinical practice, documenting numerous case studies where dream interpretation played a crucial role in the therapeutic process. These case studies illustrate how dreams can guide individuals toward resolving internal conflicts, addressing psychological traumas, and fostering a deeper understanding of their personality and life path (Jung, 1974).

Critiques and Contemporary Views: While Jung's dream analysis has been influential in psychotherapy and continues to be practiced by Jungian analysts, it has faced criticism for its subjective nature and lack of empirical evidence. Critics argue that the interpretation of dreams and symbols can be overly reliant on the therapist's intuition and may not be universally applicable (Samuels, 1985). Despite these critiques, Jung's approach to dreams remains a significant contribution to psychotherapy, offering a rich, symbolic framework for exploring the depths of the human psyche.

Therapeutic Application of Analytical Psychology

Individuation Process: At the core of Jung's therapeutic approach is the process of individuation, which Jung described as the journey toward self-realization and wholeness. This involves reconciling the conscious and unconscious aspects of the psyche, including confronting and integrating the shadow self and developing a relationship with the anima or animus. Through individuation, individuals can achieve a more balanced and harmonious inner life (Jung, 1959).

Dream Analysis: Jung considered dreams as direct expressions of the unconscious, rich with symbolic meaning. In therapy, Jungian analysts work with clients to explore and interpret dreams, uncovering insights into the client's inner world and unresolved psychological conflicts. This process can reveal underlying fears, desires, and motivations, offering pathways for psychological growth and resolution (Jung, 1974).

Active Imagination: Another key therapeutic technique in Jungian analysis is active imagination, a method that encourages clients to engage with their unconscious through imagination, visualization, or dialogue with different aspects of their psyche. This creative engagement can lead to profound insights and emotional catharsis, fostering the integration of unconscious contents (Jung, 1966).

Working with Archetypes: Jungian therapy often involves

identifying and working with archetypal themes and patterns that emerge in an individual's psyche, as expressed through dreams, fantasies, and life experiences. Recognizing these universal patterns can help individuals understand their personal experiences within a broader, more meaningful context, aiding in their psychological development (Jung, 1959).

Addressing Transference and Countertransference: In Jungian therapy, the dynamics of transference and countertransference (the emotional reactions between therapist and client) are explored as manifestations of unconscious projections. By analyzing these reactions, therapists and clients can gain insights into the clients' relational patterns and unconscious expectations, facilitating deeper self-awareness and healing (Jung, 1966).

Challenges and Ethical Considerations: While Jungian therapy offers a rich and nuanced approach to psychotherapy, it requires therapists to navigate complex symbolic material and deep psychological processes. Ethical considerations around maintaining boundaries and ensuring client safety are paramount, especially when engaging with potentially distressing unconscious content. The depth and intensity of Jungian analysis may not be suitable for all clients, highlighting the importance of tailored therapeutic approaches and the therapist's skill in navigating the unconscious (Samuels, 1985).

The therapeutic application of analytical psychology provides a profound framework for understanding and working with the unconscious, employing dream analysis, active imagination, and the exploration of archetypes to facilitate psychological healing and growth. Through the process of individuation, individuals are guided toward a more integrated and authentic self.

Critiques of Analytical Psychology

Analytical psychology has been critiqued for its lack of empirical evidence and scientific rigor. Critics argue that Jung's concepts, such as the collective unconscious and archetypes, are difficult to test and measure scientifically. Additionally, some see his theories as too mystical or esoteric, challenging their applicability in empirical psychology (Samuels, 1985).

Biography of Carl Jung

Carl Gustav Jung (1875-1961), in his quest beyond the confines of Freudian psychoanalysis, ventured into realms that were both ancient and novel. His work incorporated a wide range of human experiences and wisdom traditions, including Eastern philosophy, alchemy, Gnosticism, and indeed, Native American studies (Jung, 1964). His interest in such diverse areas wasn't just academic; it was an integral part of his understanding of the human psyche.

The Break with Freud: Initially, Jung was seen as a promising heir to Freud's psychoanalytic throne. However, their paths diverged dramatically, primarily due to Jung's rejection of Freud's theories on the primacy of sexual motivation in psychological disorders and his introduction of spiritual and mystical dimensions into analytical psychology (Jung & Freud, 1974).

Archetypes and the Collective Unconscious: Perhaps one of Jung's most enduring contributions to psychology is his theory of archetypes and the collective unconscious. Unlike the personal unconscious posited by Freud, Jung identified a deeper layer shared among individuals of the same species, housing the primordial images and symbols across cultures—the archetypes (Jung, 1959).

Individuation and Personal Growth: Jung's concept of individuation, the process of integrating the conscious with the unconscious while maintaining their relative autonomy, offers a path toward personal development and self-realization. This process is not just about self-improvement but about becoming who one truly is (Jung, 1959).

Synchronicity: Another intriguing concept introduced by Jung is synchronicity, or meaningful coincidences. Jung saw these events as significant links between the internal world of the psyche and the external physical and social world, challenging the mechanistic view of the universe (Jung, 1960).

Critiques and Misinterpretations

Over the years, Jung's ideas have been both celebrated and critiqued. The critique often centers around the perceived lack of empirical evidence supporting his theories and the esoteric nature of his work, which skeptics argue veers into the realm of pseudoscience (Shamdasani, 2003).

In recent decades, as you've noted, there's been a surge in interest in aspects of Jung's work, particularly around "shadow work." While the intention to engage with one's shadow—acknowledging and integrating the denied or suppressed parts of oneself—is valuable, it's often misinterpreted or superficially applied by those lacking a deep understanding of Jung's comprehensive framework (Jung, 1959).

Appreciating Jung Today

Despite these critiques, the richness of Jung's work and its relevance in today's world cannot be understated. His insights into the human condition, consciousness, and the structures of the psyche continue to offer profound avenues for psychological exploration and healing. Jung's legacy is not just in his theoretical contributions but in his visionary approach to understanding the complexities of the human soul.

When looking at Jung's place in history, it's clear that his work, while not without its controversies and complexities, provides a valuable perspective on the depth and breadth of the human experience. His holistic approach to psychology—encompassing the spiritual, the mystical, and the deeply personal—remains a beacon for those seeking to explore the far reaches of human consciousness.

Trait Theory/The Big Five

Dr. Hans Eysenck, PhD

Front:

Concepts: Trait Theory & The Big Five

Foundational Figures: Hans Eysenck & The Big Five Researchers

Era: Eysenck (1947), The Big Five (1980s)

Key Traits: Eysenck's Dimensions & The Big Five Traits

Core Ideas:Personality consists of broad, stable traits influencing behavior across contexts.

Eysenck's three dimensions: 1 extraversion-introversion, 2 neuroticism-stability, and 3 psychoticism.

Back:

The Big Five: 1 Openness, 2 Conscientiousness, 3 Extraversion, 4 Agreeableness, 5 Neuroticism.

Applications:Personality assessments like the Eysenck Personality Questionnaire and NEO PI-R.

Career guidance, educational strategies, and psychological research.

Critiques:Debate over the stability of traits and the influence of environmental factors.

Impact:Pioneering work in trait theory, informing research, therapy, and practical applications in various fields.

Simple Definition of Trait Theory

Trait theory posits that personality is composed of a number of broad traits, or enduring characteristics, that influence our behavior across various situations. These traits are thought to be relatively stable over time and differ from person to person (Eysenck, 1947).

Expanded Definition of Trait Theory

In the landscape of personality psychology, trait theory stands out by emphasizing the consistency of personality traits over time and across different contexts. Hans Eysenck, one of the seminal figures in this field, proposed a model of personality that centered on three major dimensions: extraversion-introversion, neuroticism-stability, and psychoticism (Eysenck, 1947). His work paved the way for subsequent models, most notably the Big Five personality traits model that emerged in the 1980s, which expanded the framework to include openness, conscientiousness, extraversion, agreeableness, and neuroticism as the foundational dimensions of personality (Costa & McCrae, 1985).

Real-World Applications of Trait Theory

Personality Assessment: Trait theory has significantly contributed to the development of personality assessments, such as the Eysenck Personality Questionnaire and the NEO Personality Inventory. These tools are widely used in psychological research, clinical settings, and even in the workplace to understand individual differences in personality (Eysenck, 1970; Costa & McCrae, 1985).

Career Guidance and Counseling: Understanding an individual's personality traits can aid in career counseling by matching personality profiles with suitable job roles. For example, high levels of openness and extraversion might be predictive of success in creative and social professions, respectively (McCrae & Costa, 1987).

Educational Applications: Teachers and educators can use trait theory to develop tailored educational strategies that cater to the diverse personality profiles of students, potentially enhancing learning outcomes and classroom management (Poropat, 2009).

Psychological Research: Trait theory provides a robust framework for exploring the relationship between personality traits and various life outcomes, including mental health, job satisfaction, and interpersonal relationships (McCrae & John, 1992).

Critiques of Trait Theory

While trait theory has been influential, it has also faced criticism for its emphasis on stability and the inherent nature of personality traits, potentially underestimating the role of the environment and situational factors in shaping behavior (Mischel, 1968). Critics argue that the theory's focus on broad traits may overlook the nuances and complexities of individual personalities.

Biography of Hans Eysenck and The Big Five

Hans Eysenck's groundbreaking work in the mid-20th century laid the foundational stones for trait theory in personality psychology. Initially controversial, Eysenck's dimensional model of personality was rooted in biological determinism, emphasizing the genetic basis of personality traits (Eysenck, 1947). Despite facing skepticism, his empirical approach to personality research has had a lasting impact on the field.

The development of the Big Five model in the 1980s represented a significant advancement in trait theory, providing a more nuanced and comprehensive framework for understanding personality. Researchers like Paul Costa and Robert McCrae expanded on earlier models, including Eysenck's, to delineate the five broad dimensions that they argued comprehensively describe human personality (Costa & McCrae, 1985).

Over time, what was once a topic of contention in psychology has become one of its most fruitful areas of study, with trait theory influencing countless research studies, psychological assessments, and practical applications in therapy, education, and beyond. Despite its critics, the evolution of trait theory from Eysenck's pioneering work to the establishment of the Big Five has underscored the importance of personality traits in understanding human behavior.

Logotherapy

Dr. Viktor Frankl MD PhD (1940s)

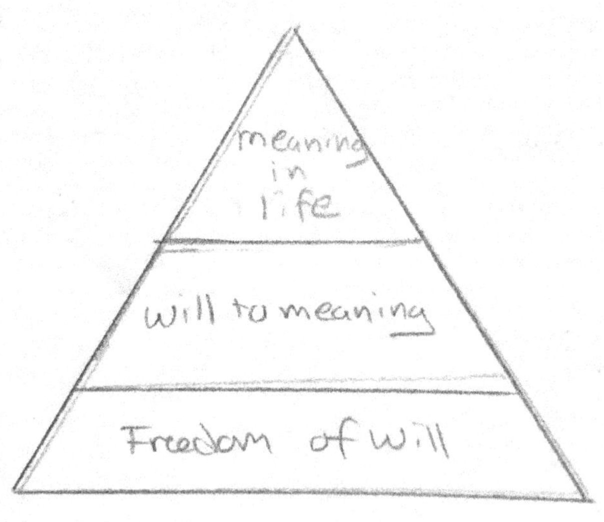

Front:

Concept: Logotherapy

Proponent: Viktor Frankl, MD, PhD

Key Insight: Focuses on the search for life's meaning as the primary motivational force.

Significance: Offers a pathway to resilience and purpose, even in profound adversity.

Back:

Core Principles:

1. Life has meaning under all circumstances.
2. Our main motivation is our will to find meaning in life.
3. Meaning can be found in work, love, and suffering, especially when facing unavoidable suffering.

Critiques: Some argue it may oversimplify the complexity of human suffering and struggle.

Simple Definition of Logotherapy

Logotherapy, developed by Viktor Frankl in the 1940s, is a form of existential therapy that emphasizes finding meaning in life as the primary motivational force for humans (Frankl, 1946). Frankl, a Holocaust survivor, argued that even in the most absurd, painful, and dehumanizing situations, life has potential meaning and that our primary drive is to discover and pursue what this meaning is for each of us individually.

Expanded Definition of Logotherapy

Building on the foundation of existential philosophy, logotherapy proposes that the search for meaning is the central human motivational force. This concept was shaped by Frankl's experiences in Nazi concentration camps, where he observed that those who could find meaning in their suffering were more likely to survive. Logotherapy is distinguished by three main principles: (1) life has meaning under all circumstances, even the most miserable ones; (2) our main motivation for living is our will to find meaning in life; and (3) we have freedom to find meaning in what we do, and what we experience, or at least in the stance we take when faced with a situation of unchangeable suffering (Frankl, 1946).

Real-World Examples of Logotherapy in Application

Resilience in Adversity: Logotherapy has illuminated paths through the darkest of life's challenges, offering not just a beacon of hope but a tangible methodology for finding purpose amidst suffering. Consider the individuals facing terminal illness or the profound grief of loss; here, Logotherapy intervenes not by diminishing the weight of their pain but by empowering them to discover a sense of meaning in their experiences (Frankl, 1959). This process of meaning-making doesn't negate their reality but rather transforms it, offering a perspective through which suffering can be seen as a source of personal growth and resilience. It's a testament to the human spirit's capacity to find light in the darkest of places, to construct purpose out of pain.

Recovery and Rehabilitation: The journey through mental health challenges—be it depression, anxiety, or PTSD—often feels like navigating an endless night. Logotherapy steps in as a guide, helping individuals to identify their unique values and to find meaning that resonates with their deepest selves (Frankl, 1959). This approach complements traditional therapeutic modalities by addressing the existential void that frequently underlies psychological turmoil. For someone ensnared in the grips of addiction, for instance, the act of uncovering personal significance can be a crucial turning point, charting a course towards recovery that is both meaningful and sustainable.

The efficacy of Logotherapy in these realms, from navigating personal trials to supporting mental health recovery, speaks to its foundational premise: that the quest for meaning is intrinsic to the human experience. However, this principle, while powerful, also invites scrutiny. The notion that meaning can be found in all circumstances, as noble as it may appear, sometimes skirts the edge of oversimplification. It raises questions about the complexity of human suffering and the variability of individual experiences (Snyder & Lopez, 2007). Can the profound depths of human despair always be countered by the search for meaning? This is the crux of my skepticism, shaped by both personal journey and professional observation.

Despite these reservations, the value of Logotherapy cannot be understated. It offers a framework not for sidestepping the realities of pain and loss but for engaging with them in a manner that seeks to uncover deeper layers of understanding and purpose. It's a dialogue, as much with oneself as with the broader existential questions of life, encouraging a relentless pursuit of meaning in the face of life's inherent challenges (Frankl, 1959).

Biography

Diving into Viktor Frankl's story, it's like stepping into a tale of resilience and existential questioning, painted against the backdrop of one of history's darkest periods. Frankl's journey, detailed in his own words in "Man's Search for Meaning" (Frankl, 1946), isn't just a survival story; it's an exploration into the depths of human endurance and the essence of finding purpose amidst profound suffering. His experiences in Nazi concentration camps laid the groundwork for Logotherapy, a beacon of hope that challenges the void of meaninglessness with the power of human will to find significance in life's every moment, especially the most torturous ones.

But here's the rub, and something I've grappled with—Frankl's Logotherapy, born from the crucible of unimaginable pain, posits that finding meaning is an intrinsic drive and a pathway to resilience (Frankl, 1959). It's an uplifting notion, sure. Yet, it carries a simplicity that sometimes feels at odds with the labyrinthine nature of personal suffering. His insistence that one can find meaning under all circumstances (Frankl, 1946) is as inspiring as it is daunting. It's a concept that, while rooted in the extremities of his life experiences, begs the question of its applicability across the diverse spectrum of human pain and despair.

Frankl's narrative is not just a chapter from a history book; it's a living dialogue with the present, reminding us of the power and potential within our quest for meaning. However, this dialogue also forces a confrontation with the theory's boundaries. Does the quest for meaning sufficiently navigate through the complexities of trauma, or does it, in its universal appeal, gloss over the individual intricacies of grief and loss?

Despite these musings, Frankl's legacy, encapsulated in "Man's Search for Meaning" and his development of Logotherapy (Frankl, 1959), remains a cornerstone of existential psychotherapy. His work transcends mere academic study, offering a philosophical compass for those adrift in the sea of existential uncertainty. Frankl didn't offer us a map but a compass—a way to orient ourselves in the pursuit of meaning, even when the stars seem dimmed by the clouds of despair.

As I reflect on Frankl and the essence of Logotherapy, it's clear that his contributions extend beyond the confines of psychology. They challenge us to engage deeply with life's most profound questions, pushing us to find our own path through suffering towards a personally defined purpose. It's a journey not of answers, but of questions; not of simplicity, but of depth.

Positive Psychology

Dr. Martin Seligman PhD (1998)

Front:

Concept: Positive Psychology

Proponent: Martin Seligman, PhD

Key Insight: Shifts psychology's focus from pathology to well-being and human strengths.

Significance: Encourages the cultivation of well-being and happiness, contributing to a fuller understanding of human potential.

Back:

Core Pillars (PERMA):

1. Positive Emotions: Fostering optimism and happiness.
2. Engagement: Being fully absorbed in activities.
3. Relationships: Building meaningful connections.
4. Meaning: Pursuing a purposeful existence.
5. Achievement: Pursuing success and mastery for its own sake.

Critiques: Critics argue it may neglect the importance of addressing negative emotions and experiences.

Simple Definition of Positive Psychology

Introduced by Martin Seligman in the late 1990s, Positive Psychology marks a shift in the focus of psychology from pathology and what goes wrong in the human mind to well-being and what makes life worth living. It's a breath of fresh air in the dense forest of psychological theories, spotlighting the potential for human flourishing and resilience rather than merely cataloging mental illnesses.

Expanded Definition of Positive Psychology

Seligman's Positive Psychology doesn't just ask how we can heal what's broken; it dares to ask how we can enhance what's already strong (Seligman, 1998). It's built on the pillars of positive emotions, engagement, relationships, meaning, and achievement—collectively known as PERMA. This framework doesn't turn a blind eye to human suffering; instead, it offers a complementary perspective, focusing on building strengths and fostering happiness as a counterbalance to life's inevitable challenges.

Real-World Examples of Positive Psychology in Application

Building Resilience: Programs and interventions grounded in Positive Psychology have been shown to bolster individuals' resilience, enabling them to bounce back more effectively from adversity. It's like psychological strength training, but for the soul.

Enhancing Well-being in Schools: Educational settings have been transformed by the infusion of Positive Psychology principles, creating environments that foster not just academic success but holistic well-being among students and staff alike.

Critiques and Contemporary Views

While the sunny outlook of Positive Psychology is appealing, it's not without its shadows. Critics argue that its focus on the positive aspects of life may overlook or minimize the complexities of human suffering and the realities of mental illness. It's a valid point—life isn't all sunshine and rainbows, and a theory that leans heavily into positivity might risk glossing over the darker, albeit essential, facets of the human experience.

Martin Seligman

Thinking on the exploration of Positive Psychology, I'm caught in a familiar push-pull of emotions. On one hand, Seligman's framework presents an invigorating departure from traditional psychology's focus on pathology, painting a picture of what psychology can aspire to achieve when it turns its lens towards human flourishing (Seligman & Csikszentmihalyi, 2000). This perspective doesn't just appeal to me; it resonates on a level that feels fundamentally hopeful. Yet, there's always that part of me that treads cautiously, wary of tipping too far into idealism without acknowledging the complexities and inevitable struggles that come with being human.

Reflecting on my formative years within the realm of psychological study, Seligman's narrative—particularly his anecdote about unsettling airplane passengers with discussions of his profession—echoes a larger discontent with how psychology, particularly under the influence of the psychoanalytic and medical models, had come to be perceived. This story, emblematic of a discipline at a crossroads, underscores a pivotal moment where psychology confronted its identity, questioning whether its focus had become too myopically aligned with dysfunction rather than the broader spectrum of human experience (Seligman, 1999).

Leading the charge as APA President, Seligman championed a reimagined purpose for psychology: to illuminate the pathways to well-being, resilience, and fulfillment. This shift towards Positive Psychology wasn't just academic; it was, and remains, a profoundly personal journey for me. The older I get, the more I witness—and participate in—the "front lines" of life, where joy and sorrow intermingle, the more I appreciate the essence of Seligman's vision. The more I see of the world, with its beauty and its bruises, the more convinced I am of the necessity of a psychology that elevates the conversation about what it means to live well (Seligman, 2011).

Seligman's approach, emphasizing strengths, virtues, and potential, offers not just a counterpoint to the deficit-focused narratives that have long dominated psychology but also a blueprint for integrating positivity into the fabric of our daily lives. It's a reminder that while the shadows of human experience are undeniable, there's immense power in directing our collective gaze towards the light—towards those elements of life that make it worth living, even in the face of adversity.

The balance Seligman advocates for—a dance between optimism and realism—is one I strive to embody. It's a philosophy that doesn't shy away from life's challenges but rather seeks to arm us with the tools to navigate them with grace, resilience, and, above all, hope. As I delve deeper into the tenets of Positive Psychology, I'm reminded that the pursuit of well-being is both a personal and a universal quest, one that requires us to hold space for the full spectrum of human emotions and experiences.

In sum, Seligman's contributions to psychology don't just resonate with me; they inspire a reevaluation of my own perspectives on happiness, resilience, and the art of living well. It's a testament to the enduring relevance of Positive Psychology and its potential to shape not only how we understand ourselves but also how we engage with the world around us.

Cognitive Behavioral Therapy (CBT)

Dr. Aaron Beck, MD (1960s)

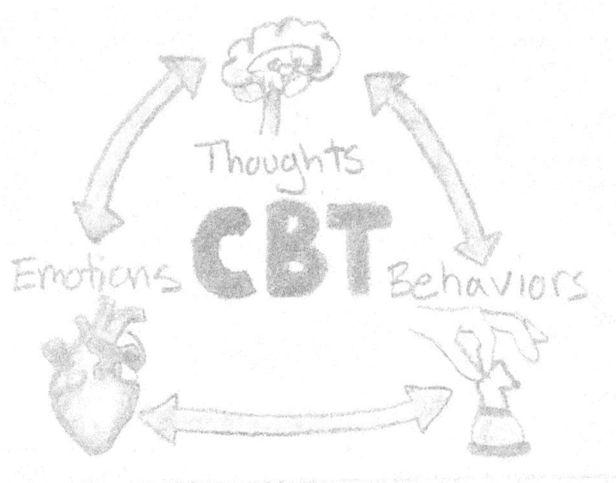

Front:

Concept: Cognitive Behavioral Therapy (CBT)

Proponent: Dr. Aaron Beck, MD

Key Insight: A therapeutic approach that addresses negative thought patterns to improve emotional regulation and develop personal coping strategies.

Significance:Evidence-based approach for mental health improvement.

Back:

Core Principles: Identification and modification of negative thoughts.

Behavioral experiments to challenge beliefs.

Skill development for emotional regulation.

Real-World Applications: Treating depression, anxiety, PTSD. Enhancing daily life coping skills.

Critiques: May overlook deeper psychological issues.

Focuses on short-term rather than long-term growth.

Simple Definition of CBT

Initially, Cognitive Behavioral Therapy (CBT), conceived by Dr. Aaron Beck in the 1960s, struck me as a venture closer to existential mysticism than to a bona fide psychological practice (Beck, 1963). The focus on modifying negative thought patterns and promoting positive self-talk seemed almost too straightforward, bordering on superficial.

Expanded Definition of CBT

However, delving deeper, CBT reveals itself as a nuanced,

empirically supported therapeutic approach, aiming to address the intricate dance between thoughts, emotions, and behaviors (Beck, 1979). This method does not merely advocate for "positive thinking" but encourages a systematic examination and restructuring of distorted cognitions, which Beck identified as the root of much psychological distress.

Real-World Examples of CBT in Application

Diving deeper into the real-world applications of Cognitive Behavioral Therapy (CBT) has significantly shifted my perspective, moving from an initial skepticism to a profound appreciation for its versatility and effectiveness. What initially seemed to be a simplistic approach to complex psychological issues has revealed itself as a deeply impactful method, capable of facilitating meaningful change in both clinical and everyday contexts.

In Mental Health Treatment: The transformative power of CBT became apparent to me through its success in addressing a wide range of mental health issues. For individuals grappling with depression, CBT has been a lifeline, offering a structured path out of the darkness. It helps patients dissect and challenge the pervasive negative thought patterns that contribute to their condition, fostering a shift towards more positive and realistic thinking (Hofmann et al., 2012). Similarly, for those suffering from anxiety disorders, CBT provides a toolkit for confronting fears head-on, rather than succumbing to avoidance or withdrawal. This approach not only alleviates symptoms but also rebuilds individuals' sense of control and efficacy in their lives. Witnessing these changes firsthand, in the lives of those I care about, underscored CBT's capacity to effect real, tangible improvements in well-being.

In Everyday Resilience: Beyond its clinical applications, CBT's influence extends into the realm of daily life, enhancing resilience against common stressors. The practice of cognitive restructuring, a key component of CBT, is particularly beneficial here. It encourages a reevaluation of stressful situations at work or in personal relationships, promoting a more balanced and constructive response to challenges. This isn't just theoretical; it's a practical skill that individuals can, and do, apply every day to navigate life's ups and downs more effectively. Through learning to identify and adjust maladaptive thought patterns, people develop a robust set of coping mechanisms that enhance their ability to deal with stress, resolve conflicts, and pursue personal goals with renewed vigor and clarity.

Reflecting on these applications of CBT, it's clear that its value extends far beyond the confines of traditional therapy sessions. Its principles offer a framework not only for healing but for living more fully, embodying a proactive stance towards mental health and well-being. The journey from skepticism to advocacy for CBT underscores a broader narrative about the power of evidence-based psychological practices to transform lives—not just in moments of crisis, but every single day.

Critiques and Contemporary Views

Despite my evolved view, it's crucial to acknowledge the critiques. Some argue that CBT's focus on the individual's cognitions may overlook the broader social and environmental factors influencing mental health (Wampold, 2001). This critique resonates, highlighting the importance of a balanced approach that considers both internal and external determinants of well-being.

Biography

Dr. Aaron Beck's journey into the realm of psychology wasn't just a career choice; it was a revolution in the making. When Beck introduced Cognitive Behavioral Therapy (CBT) in the 1960s, the field of psychology was entrenched in Freudian psychoanalysis and behaviorism. Beck, however, charted a new course, one that would eventually reshape the landscape of psychotherapeutic practices (Beck, 1963).

Initially trained in psychoanalysis, Beck's own empirical research led him to question the psychoanalytic doctrines of the day. His curiosity and relentless pursuit of evidence-based practices drove him to develop CBT, fundamentally altering our approach to mental health treatment (Beck, 1964). It wasn't just his groundbreaking work in depression that set him apart; it was his unwavering belief in the power of the scientific method to uncover the mechanisms of the mind (Beck, 1979).

Beck's contributions extend beyond the creation of CBT. He pioneered the use of "automatic thoughts" to explain how our perceptions of the world influence our emotional responses. This concept, simple yet profound, has become a cornerstone in understanding and treating psychological distress (Beck et al., 1979).

Yet, to speak of Beck merely in terms of his professional

achievements is to miss the essence of the man. Beck's legacy is not just in the therapies he developed but in the countless lives transformed by his work. His approach to psychology was revolutionary not because it was radical but because it was rational. In a field rife with abstract theories, Beck sought clarity, precision, and accessibility.

Reflecting on Dr. Aaron Beck's legacy, I'm struck by the profound humanity of his work. His dedication to evidence-based treatment and his compassion for those suffering from mental illness have left an indelible mark on the field of psychology. Beck's journey from a psychoanalyst to the father of CBT is a testament to the power of questioning, research, and innovation.

Beck's work serves as a beacon, guiding us toward a more compassionate, effective, and scientifically grounded approach to mental health. His legacy, characterized by both brilliance and humility, continues to inspire a new generation of psychologists and therapists—a legacy as enduring as the principles of CBT itself.

My journey from skepticism to advocacy for CBT mirrors a broader journey of understanding in psychology. What once seemed like an oversimplified solution has unveiled itself as a cornerstone of psychological intervention, capable of profound impact. This transformation in perspective, partly nurtured by personal loss and the influence of my dearly departed fiancée, has underscored the value of CBT not just as a therapeutic tool but as a vital component of psychological resilience and healing.

Cognitive Development (Developmental Psychology)

Dr. Jean Piaget, PhD (1920s)

Front:

Concept: Cognitive Development

Proponent: Dr. Jean Piaget, PhD

Key Insight: Piaget's theory revolutionized understanding of child cognitive development.

Back:

Definition: Piaget's theory explains how children develop thinking skills.

Stages: 1 Sensorimotor, 2Preoperational,3 Concrete Operational, 4 Formal Operational.

Impact: Influential in education and psychology.

Simple Definition of Cognitive Development

Cognitive development refers to the progression of learning, problem-solving, and decision-making abilities from infancy through adulthood. Jean Piaget's seminal work in the 1920s established a framework suggesting that cognitive growth occurs in a series of stages, each marked by distinct cognitive capabilities and ways of interacting with the world (Piaget, 1952).

Expanded Definition of Cognitive Development

Building on the foundational concept, Piaget's theory of cognitive development detailed the process as a sequence of four main stages: the Sensorimotor Stage, Preoperational Stage, Concrete Operational Stage, and Formal Operational Stage. This theory underscores the idea that children actively construct their understanding of the world through direct interactions with their environment, emphasizing the role of maturation, experience, social interaction, and equilibration in cognitive development. According to Piaget, these stages reflect the increasing sophistication of children's thought processes and their ability to understand complex concepts and abstract reasoning over time. Central to this theory is the belief that cognitive development is not just about acquiring more information but involves fundamental changes in how children think, understand, and perceive the world around them (Piaget, 1964).

Real-World Examples of Cognitive Development

Building on the foundational concept, Piaget's theory of cognitive development detailed the process as a sequence of four main stages: the Sensorimotor Stage, Preoperational Stage, Concrete Operational Stage, and Formal Operational Stage.

1. Sensorimotor Stage: This stage, spanning from birth to around two years of age, is characterized by infants' exploration of the world through sensory experiences and motor actions. Key milestones include the development of object permanence—the understanding that objects continue to exist even when they are not visible—and the emergence of basic forms of symbolic thought.

1. Preoperational Stage: From approximately ages two to seven, children enter the preoperational stage, marked

by the development of language and symbolic thinking. However, they still lack the ability to perform operations, such as mental transformations or conservation tasks. Their thinking tends to be egocentric, meaning they struggle to consider perspectives other than their own.

1. Concrete Operational Stage: Between the ages of seven and eleven, children enter the concrete operational stage, during which they begin to grasp concepts such as conservation, reversibility, and the ability to perform logical operations, albeit in concrete, tangible contexts. Their thinking becomes less egocentric, and they can understand viewpoints other than their own.

1. Formal Operational Stage: Beginning around age eleven and continuing into adulthood, individuals reach the formal operational stage. In this stage, abstract thinking and hypothetical reasoning abilities emerge. They can engage in deductive reasoning, systematically explore possibilities, and think about hypothetical situations and abstract concepts.

Piaget's theory underscores the idea that children actively construct their understanding of the world through direct interactions with their environment, emphasizing the role of maturation, experience, social interaction, and equilibration in cognitive development. According to Piaget, these stages reflect the increasing sophistication of children's thought processes and their ability to understand complex concepts and abstract reasoning over time. Central to this theory is the belief that cognitive development is not just about acquiring more information but involves fundamental changes in how children think, understand, and perceive the world around them (Piaget, 1964).

Piaget's theory, while foundational, has not been without its critics. Researchers have contested Piaget's estimation of children's cognitive abilities, arguing that the developmental stages might be more fluid and less universal than Piaget posited. Furthermore, critiques have emerged regarding the theory's limited consideration of cultural and social influences on cognitive development, suggesting a more context-dependent view of learning (Vygotsky, 1978).

Biography

Dr. Jean Piaget, a Swiss psychologist, revolutionized our under-standing of cognitive development with his groundbreaking work in the 1920s. His contributions to psychology cannot be overstated. As someone who has spent considerable time interacting with younger children, I've found Piaget's theories to be not just insightful but also incredibly practical. His theories provide a framework for understanding how children learn, think, and perceive the world around them.

Piaget's research emphasized the active role of children in constructing their knowledge through interactions with their environment. This concept resonates deeply with me, as I've witnessed firsthand the curiosity and exploration that children engage in as they navigate their surroundings. Piaget's stages of cognitive development, from the sensorimotor stage to the formal operational stage, offer valuable insights into the progression of children's cognitive abilities and how they make sense of the world.

In my experience, Piaget's theories have practical applications in various settings, from childcare and education to parenting and psychology. Understanding Piaget's stages of development can inform teaching strategies, curriculum design, and parenting approaches. By aligning activities and learning experiences with children's developmental stages, educators and caregivers can support optimal learning and growth.

For anyone studying psychology or working with children, familiarity with Piaget's theories is essential. His work forms the foundation of developmental psychology and continues to influence research and practice in the field. Whether you're a parent, teacher, or aspiring psychologist, delving into Piaget's theories offers valuable insights into the fascinating journey of cognitive development.

Piaget's legacy lives on in the countless individuals whose lives have been touched by his work. His theories remain as relevant today as they were decades ago, serving as a guiding light for understanding the complex process of human development. As I reflect on my own experiences with children and psychology, I'm grateful for Piaget's contributions and the enduring impact they've had on our understanding of cognitive development.

Engaging with Piaget's theory offers invaluable insights into the intricate process of learning and adaptation. His view of learners as active participants in their cognitive development—though revolutionary at the time—echoes in modern educational philosophies that emphasize exploratory and hands-on learning. Piaget's work underscores the importance of nurturing environments that foster, rather than inhibit, the innate curiosity and intelligence that drive cognitive development.

Psychosocial Development

Dr. Erik Erikson, PhD (1950s)

Front:

Concept: Psychosocial Development

Theorist: Erik Erikson, PhD

Framework Introduced: 1950s

Key Insight: Human development is characterized by eight stages, each marked by a specific psychosocial conflict.

Development occurs throughout the lifespan, from infancy to old age.

Each stage involves a fundamental conflict that must be resolved for healthy psychological development.

Back:

Significant Stages:

1. Trust vs. Mistrust (Infancy)
2. Autonomy vs. Shame and Doubt (Early Childhood)
3. Initiative vs. Guilt (Preschool Age)
4. Industry vs. Inferiority (School Age)
5. Identity vs. Role Confusion (Adolescence)
6. Intimacy vs. Isolation (Young Adulthood)
7. Generativity vs. Stagnation (Middle Adulthood)
8. Integrity vs. Despair (Late Adulthood)

Applications: Influential in education, therapy, and counseling, providing a framework for understanding and supporting individuals at different life stages.

Critiques: While widely influential, Erikson's theory has been critiqued for its potential lack of applicability across diverse cultures and the evolving challenges of the modern world.

Simple Definition of Psychosocial Development

Erikson's theory of psychosocial development revolutionized our understanding of human growth, positing that development occurs across eight distinct stages throughout the lifespan, each marked by a specific psychosocial conflict (Erikson, 1950). This framework expanded psychoanalytic theory beyond Freud's initial focus, integrating societal and cultural dimensions into the formation of identity and personality.

Expanded Definition of Psychosocial Development

At the heart of Erikson's theory is the notion that each stage of development is characterized by a fundamental conflict serving as a critical juncture in an individual's psychosocial development (Erikson, 1950). From trust vs. mistrust in infancy to integrity vs. despair in old age, Erikson delineated how each stage presents unique challenges and opportunities for personal growth, emphasizing the continuous interaction between the individual and their social environment (Erikson, 1959).

Real-World Examples of Psychosocial Development in Application

Educational Settings: Erikson's theory has a profound impact on educational practices, particularly in understanding and addressing the psychosocial needs of students at different developmental stages. For instance, during the "industry versus inferiority" stage, which typically occurs during the elementary school years, educators can foster an environment that encourages mastery and competence. By assigning tasks that are challenging yet achievable, teachers can promote industry, helping children develop a sense of capability and self-confidence (Erikson, 1963). This approach aligns with research suggesting that early academic success is a critical predictor of future educational attainment and self-esteem (Masten et al., 2005).

Therapy and Counseling: In therapeutic settings, Erikson's stages provide a framework for understanding clients' issues through the lens of psychosocial development. Therapists can use this model to identify and address crises that may have arisen from unresolved conflicts in earlier stages. For example, during adolescence, the challenge of "identity versus role confusion" becomes paramount. Therapists working with teenagers can focus on identity exploration, offering guidance as they navigate the complexities of role experimentation and self-discovery (Erikson, 1968). This is supported by literature indicating that successful navigation of this stage is crucial for the formation of a coherent and stable adult identity (Kroger & Marcia, 2011).

Workplace Dynamics: Erikson's theory also extends to understanding dynamics in the workplace, particularly in the context of "generativity versus stagnation," a stage that typically concerns adults in middle age. Employers can create opportunities for mentorship and innovation, allowing employees to contribute meaningfully to the organization and, by extension, to society. This not only promotes workplace satisfaction but also addresses the generative needs of this developmental stage (McAdams & de St. Aubin, 1998).

Community and Social Engagement: The application of Erikson's stages can further be seen in community and social settings, where initiatives that promote engagement and social responsibility resonate with the need for generativity. Programs that encourage volunteerism and community service can provide outlets for individuals seeking to achieve a sense of contribution and connection, reflecting the theory's emphasis on the importance of societal roles in development (Snarey, 1993).

Critiques and Contemporary Views

Despite its widespread influence, Erikson's theory has been critiqued for its potential lack of applicability across diverse cultures and the evolving challenges of the digital age. Critics argue that the stages, conceptualized in the mid-20th century, may not fully account for the nuanced processes of identity formation in today's globalized society (Côté & Levine, 2002).

Biography of Erik Erikson

Erik Erikson's journey through the world of psychology was not just an academic pursuit but a deeply personal exploration of identity and society. Born in 1902, Erikson's own search for a sense of belonging and purpose mirrored the stages of development he would later theorize (Erikson, 1950; 1968). His work transcended the boundaries of traditional psychoanalysis to incorporate a broader understanding of the cultural, social, and historical forces shaping human identity.

Erikson's theory of psychosocial development, with its eight distinct stages, has become a foundational element in understanding human growth. His innovative approach introduced the idea that development continues throughout the lifespan, with each stage presenting new challenges and opportunities for growth (Erikson, 1950). This perspective was revolutionary, emphasizing the role of societal influences and the ongoing nature of identity formation.

Reflecting on Erikson's contributions, I am struck by the depth and nuance of his understanding of the human condition. His stages of development offer a lens through which to view our own lives, encouraging a reflective engagement with the core challenges we face at different times. From the trust versus mistrust of infancy to the integrity versus despair of old age, Erikson's work illuminates the path of human experience, highlighting the search for meaning and connection that defines our existence.

Erikson's own life story is a testament to the theory he espoused. His diverse background and experiences provided a rich tapestry from which he drew his insights into identity and development. As a teacher, artist, and psychoanalyst, Erikson navigated multiple worlds, embodying the very process of identity exploration and integration that he described in his stages (Friedman, 1999). His work with children and adolescents, in particular, demonstrated his profound empathy and understanding of the struggles inherent in the process of becoming.

On a personal level, Erikson's theory resonates with me as a useful framework for understanding not just the challenges we face but the potential for growth and transformation inherent in each stage of life. His emphasis on the psychosocial aspects of development highlights the interconnectedness of individual experience and social context, reminding us that our journey through life is shaped by a complex interplay of internal and external forces.

Erikson's legacy is not merely academic; it is a living, breathing guide to understanding ourselves and others. His work challenges us to consider how we navigate the crises and transitions of our lives, offering insights that are as relevant today as they were when he first articulated them. In reflecting on Erikson's life and contributions, I am inspired by his ability to blend theory and practice, intellect and empathy, in a manner that speaks to the enduring quest for identity and meaning that defines the human experience.

Neo-Freudian Psychoanalysis

Dr. Karen Horney, MD (1940s)

Front:

Concept: Neo-Freudian Psychoanalysis

Key Figure: Karen Horney

Focus: Emphasizes social and cultural factors in personality development and neurosis.

Impact:Paved the way for feminist psychology and humanistic approaches.

Influenced therapeutic practices by focusing on the individual's social context

Back:

Core Ideas:Basic anxiety as the root of neurosis.

Challenges to Freud's theories, particularly regarding sexuality and female psychology.

Introduction of interpersonal strategies to cope with anxiety: moving towards, against, or away from people.

Significance: Horney's work represents a critical shift in psychoanalytic theory, advocating for the importance of cultural and environmental influences on psychological well-being.

Simple Definition of Neo-Freudian Psychoanalysis

Neo-Freudian psychoanalysis marks a departure from traditional Freudian concepts by prioritizing the influence of social and cultural factors over innate instincts in personality development and the genesis of neurosis. It introduces the notion of basic anxiety as central to understanding neurosis, emphasizing the critical role of interpersonal relationships and cultural contexts (Horney, 1945).

Expanded Theory

This psychoanalytic approach expands the framework for psychological development to assert that neuroses primarily result from environmental and cultural pressures rather than solely from unresolved unconscious conflicts or early childhood experiences (Horney, 1950). It elaborates on coping mechanisms individuals employ, such as moving towards, against, or away from people, as strategies to manage basic anxiety. These strategies underscore the adaptive responses individuals have towards their social surroundings, demonstrating the nuanced ways in which people navigate their environments to maintain psychological health (Horney, 1945; 1950).

Real-World Examples of Neo-Freudian Psychoanalysis in Application

Karen Horney's Neo-Freudian psychoanalysis has significantly influenced various domains, offering insights into human behavior, neurosis treatment, and the impact of societal structures on individual psychology.

Therapeutic Practices: Horney's theories have reshaped therapeutic approaches by focusing on the individual's social context and interpersonal relationships as key factors in understanding and treating neurosis. Her emphasis on basic anxiety and the ten neurotic needs provides therapists with a framework to explore the underlying causes of their patients' distress, facilitating more personalized and effective treatment strategies (Quinn, 2013). This approach allows for a broader exploration of the patient's life, including cultural and environmental influences, expanding the scope of psychotherapy beyond the confines of traditional Freudian analysis.

Feminist Psychology: Horney is considered a pioneer in feminist psychology for challenging Freud's views on female psychology and introducing the concept of womb envy, a counterpoint to penis envy, which suggests that men may experience envy towards women's reproductive capabilities (Horney, 1967). Her critique of the patriarchal biases in Freudian theory has encouraged subsequent generations of psychologists to examine how gender and power dynamics influence psychological development and pathology, contributing to a more nuanced understanding of gender-related issues in psychology (Westkott, 1993).

Sociocultural Analyses: Beyond the clinical setting, Horney's theories have been applied to understand the psychological impact of cultural and social conditions. Her insights into the ways social environments influence personality development have informed studies on cultural identity, social alienation, and the psychological effects of sexism and racism (Horney, 1950; Paris, 1994). This aspect of her work highlights the interaction between individual psychology and societal structures, offering valuable perspectives for sociologists, anthropologists, and cultural psychologists.

Educational Implications: Horney's focus on the social roots of neurosis and the importance of healthy interpersonal relationships has implications for educational psychology, particularly in designing supportive learning environments that promote psychological well-being. Understanding the role of basic anxiety in learning difficulties or social behavior in schools can lead educators to implement strategies that foster a sense of security and belonging among students (Kellogg, 2000).

Critiques and Contemporary Views

While Horney's contributions significantly advanced psycho-analytic thought, some critics argue that her emphasis on cultural and environmental factors might underplay the role of biological and unconscious processes in psychological development. Despite this, her work remains a cornerstone of humanistic psychology and psychoanalytic theory, offering a more balanced view of the forces that shape the human psyche.

Biography

Exploring the life and work of Karen Horney, I find myself drawn not just to her intellectual contributions but to her spirit of rebellion. It's refreshing to see someone so fearlessly challenge the established norms of her time, particularly within the male-dominated field of psychoanalysis. Horney's defiance against Freudian orthodoxy not only marks her as a pioneering figure in psychology but also as a symbol of challenging the status quo (Quinn, 2013). This aspect of her persona resonates with me deeply; there's something inherently compelling about individuals who dare to question and redefine the boundaries of their disciplines.

It's intriguing how often Horney is highlighted primarily as a 'female psychologist,' especially considering that women now significantly outnumber men in the field of psychology. This shift in demographics underscores the changing landscape of psychology, yet Horney's legacy reminds us that breaking new ground often involves challenging deeply entrenched beliefs, regardless of one's gender (Westkott, 1993).

Her work strikes a chord similar to the themes explored in beloved old television shows like Cheers and Frasier—where the underdog or the unconventional often provides the most profound insights. While I maintain a healthy skepticism towards both Neo-Freudian and Freudian theories, I can't help but appreciate Horney's contributions to expanding upon Freud's work. Her critiques and subsequent theories offer a fascinating twist on the Great Man Theory, suggesting that great ideas can come from anyone willing to critically engage with and challenge existing paradigms (Horney, 1950; Paris, 1994).

Karen Horney's exploration of neurosis, her development of theories around basic anxiety, and her critique of Freud's views on women not only advanced psychoanalytic theory but also paved the way for subsequent generations to further explore the psychological impacts of societal and cultural constructs (Horney, 1945; 1950). This makes her work not just a footnote in the history of psychology but a cornerstone for those who seek to understand the intricate dance between individual psychology and broader social influences.

Karen Horney's legacy is not merely in her defiance or her gender, but in her enduring contributions to the field of psychology. She exemplifies how challenging the status quo can lead to significant advancements and deeper understandings, a lesson that remains as relevant today as it was in her time.

Social Learning Theory

Dr. Albert Bandura, PhD (1960s)

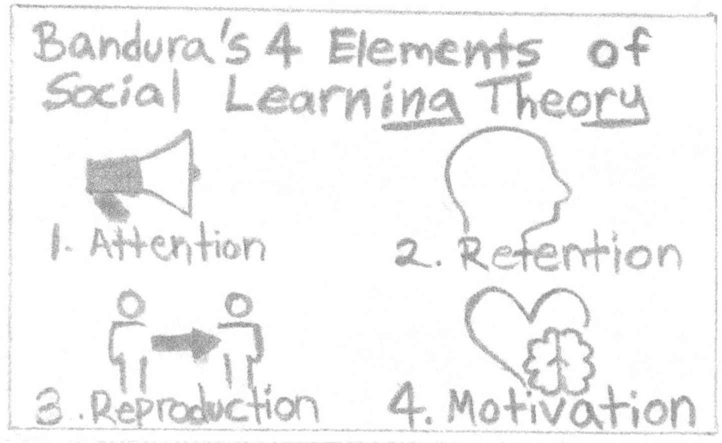

Front:

Concept: Social Learning Theory

Key Figure: Albert Bandura

Focus: Learning through observation and imitation.

Impact: Influential in educational psychology, emphasizing the importance of role models.

Highlights the media's role in shaping behavior, sparking debates on media violence.

Informs therapeutic practices, utilizing modeling for behavior modification.

Back:

Core Ideas: Learning occurs within a social context, not just through direct experience.

Emphasizes the role of modeling, observation, and imitation in acquiring new behaviors.

Introduces vicarious reinforcement: learning from the consequences of others' actions.

Critiques: Some argue it underestimates biological factors in behavior.

Critics question the simplification of complex human cognition and behavior.

Simple Definition of Social Learning Theory

Social Learning Theory posits that learning occurs within a social context, emphasizing that individuals can acquire new behaviors through observation and imitation of others, even without direct reinforcement. This concept broadens the traditional understanding of learning to include vicarious experiences as a fundamental component of the learning process (Bandura, 1971).

Expanded Definition of Social Learning Theory

Central to Social Learning Theory is the notion of observational learning, where the actions of others serve as a guide for new behaviors. The theory introduces the idea of vicarious reinforcement, suggesting that seeing others rewarded or punished for certain behaviors can influence an individual's likelihood of adopting similar behaviors. This approach to learning highlights the significant role of models in the social environment and the cognitive processes involved in observing and replicating behaviors (Bandura, 1977).

Application of Social Learning Theory

Educational Implications: Social Learning Theory has revolutionized educational practices by highlighting the significance of observational learning and modeling in the classroom. The theory suggests that teachers and peers serve as influential models, demonstrating behaviors and attitudes that students are likely to imitate (Bandura, 1986). This insight has led to the development of instructional strategies that leverage modeling for educational purposes, including the use of role-playing and simulation games to teach complex concepts and social skills. Such approaches facilitate a learning environment where students can observe and practice desired behaviors in a supportive setting, improving both academic and social outcomes (Schunk, 2012).

Influence on Media and Behavior: The theory's exploration

of media's role in shaping behavior underscores the powerful effect that televised and online behaviors can have on viewers, particularly children. Bandura's research into the effects of media violence on aggression demonstrated that individuals could learn and replicate aggressive behaviors observed in media content (Bandura, 2001). This understanding has informed policy discussions and interventions aimed at mitigating the negative impacts of media violence, emphasizing the need for media literacy programs that teach critical viewing skills and the selection of appropriate content.

Therapeutic and Behavior Modification Practices: Social Learning Theory has been instrumental in developing therapeutic techniques that utilize modeling and observation for behavior change. In treating phobias, anxiety disorders, and various maladaptive behaviors, therapists often employ modeling as a technique for demonstrating healthy behaviors and coping strategies (Bandura, 1969). This method allows individuals to learn through the success of others without having to first undergo direct exposure to stressful stimuli, providing a safe and effective means of modifying behavior.

Workplace Training and Development: The application of Social Learning Theory extends into the workplace, where modeling and vicarious learning are used to train and develop employees. By observing the successful performance of tasks by peers or mentors, employees can acquire new skills and knowledge, enhancing their competence and confidence in their roles (Bandura, 1977). This approach underscores the importance of creating a culture of learning and mentorship within organizations, where positive behaviors and practices are actively demonstrated and shared.

Promoting Health and Public Health Campaigns: Social Learning Theory has also been applied in designing public health campaigns that aim to change health-related behaviors. By showcasing positive health behaviors and the benefits of such practices through media and public figures, these campaigns leverage observational learning to encourage healthier lifestyle choices among the public (Bandura, 2004).

Critiques of Social Learning Theory

Underestimation of Biological Factors: One of the primary critiques of Social Learning Theory is its perceived underestimation of the role of biological factors in human behavior and learning. Critics argue that by focusing predominantly on environmental and observational influences, the theory may neglect innate biological predispositions that significantly shape behavior (Skinner, 1974). For instance, tendencies towards aggression or specific phobias might be more deeply rooted in an individual's genetic makeup than in their social learning experiences, suggesting a need for a more integrated approach that considers both biological and environmental factors (Pinker, 2002).

Oversimplification of Human Cognition: Critics also contend that Social Learning Theory oversimplifies the complexity of human cognition. The theory emphasizes imitation and modeling as primary mechanisms of learning, potentially overlooking the nuanced cognitive processes involved in decision-making, reasoning, and problem-solving. This critique highlights the need for models of learning that more fully account for the diverse cognitive capacities that contribute to how individuals interpret and respond to their environments (Baumeister & Vohs, 2004).

Limited Scope in Explaining Complex Behaviors: While Social Learning Theory has been influential in explaining a wide range of behaviors, critics suggest that it may have a limited scope in accounting for more complex behaviors that are influenced by a multitude of factors beyond mere observation and imitation. Complex social behaviors, such as altruism, empathy, or moral reasoning, may require a broader theoretical framework that encompasses emotional, ethical, and cognitive dimensions beyond the scope of Social Learning Theory (Haidt, 2001).

Challenges in Media Influence Research: In applying Social Learning Theory to understand the impact of media on behavior, particularly concerning aggression, critics point to the challenges in isolating observational learning from other variables. The relationship between media consumption and aggressive behavior is complex, influenced by individual differences, contextual factors, and media content nuances. Some research suggests that the effects of media violence may be less direct and more conditional than Social Learning Theory implies, calling for a more nuanced exploration of how individuals interact with and are influenced by media (Ferguson & Kilburn, 2009).

Critiques and Contextualization of Bobo Doll Experiments

One of the most emblematic demonstrations of Social Learning

Theory is Albert Bandura's Bobo doll experiment, which played a pivotal role in illustrating how children imitate aggressive behaviors observed in adults (Bandura, Ross, & Ross, 1961). In these experiments, children who observed an adult model acting aggressively towards a Bobo doll were more likely to also exhibit aggressive behaviors towards the doll, compared to children who had not been exposed to the aggressive model. This research provided compelling empirical support for the theory's assertion that behaviors can be learned through observation, even in the absence of direct reinforcement.

Influence of Media Violence: The experiments have been central to debates on the impact of media violence on children's behavior. Critics suggest that the straightforward link between observed aggression and imitation seen in the experiments oversimplifies the relationship between media consumption and aggressive behavior in children. They argue that individual differences, such as temperament, and contextual factors, like family environment, play significant roles in mediating the effects of observed violence (Ferguson & Kilburn, 2009).

Generalization to Real-world Aggression: While the Bobo doll experiments significantly advanced the understanding of observational learning, some researchers caution against directly equating the imitation of aggression in a controlled setting with real-world aggression and violence. The capacity for moral reasoning, empathy, and the understanding of social norms are among factors that influence how observed behaviors are interpreted and whether they are acted upon in real life (Haidt, 2001; Pinker, 2002).

Biography and Reflection - Albert Bandura: A Behavioralist's Behavioralist

What can I say? I've always had a soft spot for behavioralists, and Albert Bandura, emerging from that golden age of psychology, provided a refreshing counterpoint to the dense forest of psychoanalytic models. There's something to be said about the straightforward appeal of observing behavior and saying, "Yep, that's how we learn." Bandura, with his Social Learning Theory, did just that—albeit, some of my more avant-garde professors thought his theories a bit passé, echoing a sentiment that by the turn of the 21st century, we were all a tad weary of hearing the same old behavioral spiel.

Yet, Bandura's legacy, especially his iconic Bobo Doll Experiment, left an indelible mark on my academic upbringing. That study, seared into my brain in the early days of my psychology education, seemed to underline in bold the notion that we're all just a product of what we see and imitate (Bandura, Ross, & Ross, 1961). But here's where my fondness for Bandura gets complicated. The media's misuse of his work to argue that video games spawn generations of violence always struck me as a misinterpretation of his findings—a distortion that neglects the nuanced, multifaceted nature of human behavior and the myriad influences shaping it.

Diving deeper into the realms of psychology and sociology, I've come to appreciate the intricate dance between the individual and society that Bandura's work highlights. It's a prime example of how sociology and psychology are not just adjacent fields but deeply intertwined, each informing the other in the study of personality and social structures. His work, while seemingly stating the obvious—yes, the people around us influence us— was, in its time, a necessary quantification of social influences on behavior, paving the way for further exploration into the social fabric of learning and development (Bandura, 1977).

However, I can't help but chuckle at the notion of Bandura's findings being labeled "groundbreaking" for essentially pointing out that humans influence each other. It seems akin to applauding Freud for allowing people to talk about their feelings—a bit of a "Well, duh" moment in hindsight. Yet, acknowledging this doesn't diminish Bandura's contributions; it simply places them in a context that recognizes the evolution of psychological thought and the sometimes cyclical nature of what we deem revolutionary. And I have little room level criticism.

As for Bandura's work not delving deeply into phobias, PTSD, and the like, it's a reminder of the temporal limitations of any scientific endeavor. The fields of psychology and sociology continually evolve, building upon the foundations laid by thinkers like Bandura to explore new territories and challenges (Bandura, 1986). His work, foundational yet ripe for further exploration, underscores the dynamic interplay of observation, imitation, and the myriad other factors..

While I may joke around about the "earth-shattering" revelations of Social Learning Theory, I hold a deep respect for Bandura's contributions. His research has not only illuminated the paths of social influence and learning but also underscored the importance of empirical evidence in shaping our understanding of human behavior. He passed away in 2021, And yes, there's always more to read, more to question—a testament to the enduring intrigue of Bandura's work in personality theory.

Field Theory

Dr. Kurt Lewin, PhD (1930s)

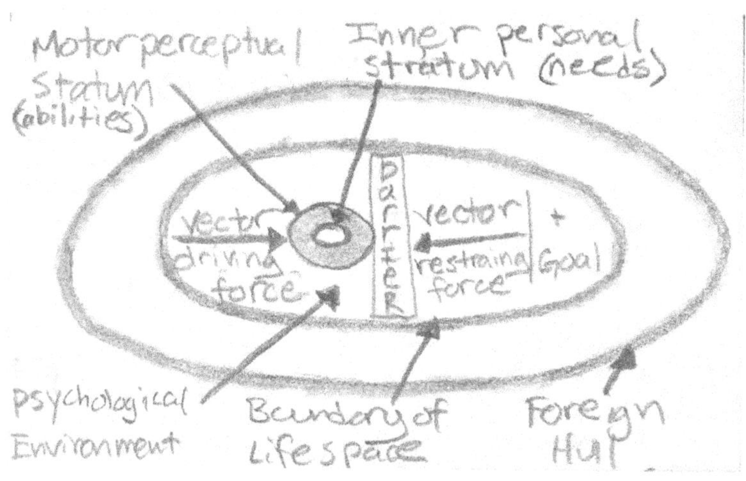

Front:

Concept: Field Theory

Key Figure: Kurt Lewin

Era: 1930s

Key Principle: Behavior = Function(Person, Environment)

Core Ideas:Behavior is the result of dynamic interactions within the "life space."

Emphasizes psychological and environmental forces.

Back:

Impact:Change management in organizational development.

Insights into group dynamics and leadership in social psychology.

Influences on educational strategies.

Critiques:Abstract nature complicates empirical testing.

Calls for broader integration of factors influencing behavior.

Simple Definition of Field Theory

Field Theory, introduced by Kurt Lewin in the 1930s, posits that human behavior is the result of the dynamic interactions between individuals and their environments. The theory emphasizes the "field" or "life space" in which these interactions occur, suggesting that behavior cannot be fully understood without considering the totality of the psychological and situational forces acting upon an individual at any given time (Lewin, 1936).

Expanded Definition of Field Theory

At the core of Field Theory is the concept of the life space, which encompasses all the internal and external forces influencing an individual's behavior. Lewin proposed that behavior (B) is a function of the person (P) and their environment (E), often summarized as $B = f(P, E)$. This equation underscores Lewin's belief in the interdependence of psychological factors and external conditions in shaping behavior. Field Theory introduced methodologies for mapping these forces and their effects, offering a systematic approach to analyzing and predicting behavior within specific contexts (Lewin, 1951).

Applications and Impact of Field Theory:

Kurt Lewin's Field Theory has had profound implications across various domains of psychology and related fields, emphasizing the dynamic relationship between individuals and their environments. This theory has not only advanced our understanding of human behavior but also provided practical frameworks for addressing real-world issues.

Organizational Development: Lewin's Field Theory underpins his three-step model of organizational change (unfreezing, change, and refreezing), which has become a cornerstone in change management practices. By analyzing the forces within an organization's field, leaders can strategically plan and implement effective change initiatives. This approach helps in identifying and overcoming resistance to change, ensuring that new behaviors are solidified within the organizational culture (Lewin, 1947).

Social Psychology: Lewin's work laid the groundwork for

modern social psychology, particularly in the study of group dynamics, leadership styles, and decision-making processes. Field Theory has been applied to understand how group norms and roles influence individual behavior, offering insights into effective team management and conflict resolution strategies. It also informs the development of interventions aimed at fostering social change and improving group relations (Lewin, 1951).

Educational Psychology: In education, Lewin's concepts have informed strategies to create more effective learning environments. Understanding the life space of students allows educators to tailor educational approaches that address both academic and emotional needs, thereby enhancing motivation and learning outcomes. Field Theory also supports the development of classroom management techniques that consider the psychological field of the classroom, promoting a positive and conducive learning atmosphere (Lewin, 1936).

Clinical Psychology and Therapy: Lewin's principles have influenced therapeutic practices by highlighting the importance of considering the client's life space in the therapeutic process. Therapists can use Field Theory to explore the complex interplay of personal and environmental factors affecting clients, guiding interventions that address the broader context of clients' lives. This holistic approach facilitates more comprehensive and effective treatment plans (Lewin, 1951).

Community and Social Change: Lewin's commitment to applying psychological research to solve societal problems led to the development of action research, a method that combines theory and practice to promote social change. By engaging directly with communities to understand their fields and implement interventions, psychologists can work collaboratively with stakeholders to effect meaningful and sustainable change (Lewin, 1946).

The breadth of Field Theory's applications and its impact across different areas underscore Kurt Lewin's legacy as a visionary thinker whose ideas continue to resonate. By focusing on the totality of the field in which behavior occurs, Lewin's work encourages a holistic and nuanced understanding of human behavior, offering valuable insights and tools for researchers, practitioners, and policymakers alike.

Critiques of Field Theory:

Despite its contributions, Field Theory has been critiqued for its abstract concepts and the challenge of empirical validation. Critics argue that the subjective nature of the life space and the complexity of psychological fields make it difficult to test Lewin's theories rigorously (Marrow, 1969).

Legacy of Kurt Lewin:

Kurt Lewin is celebrated as a pioneer in social psychology, whose introduction of Field Theory offered a novel lens through which to view the complexities of human behavior. His interdisciplinary approach bridged psychology with sociology and organizational studies, leaving an indelible mark on the social sciences (Lewin, 1948).Kurt Lewin's legacy is characterized by his innovative approaches to understanding human behavior and his unwavering belief in the application of psychological research for the betterment of society. His work continues to inspire and challenge psychologists, educators, and social scientists to explore the dynamic interactions between individuals and their environments. Lewin's contributions have left an indelible mark on the field of psychology, demonstrating the enduring relevance of his theories and methodologies.

Existential Psychology

Dr. Rollo May, PhD (1950s)

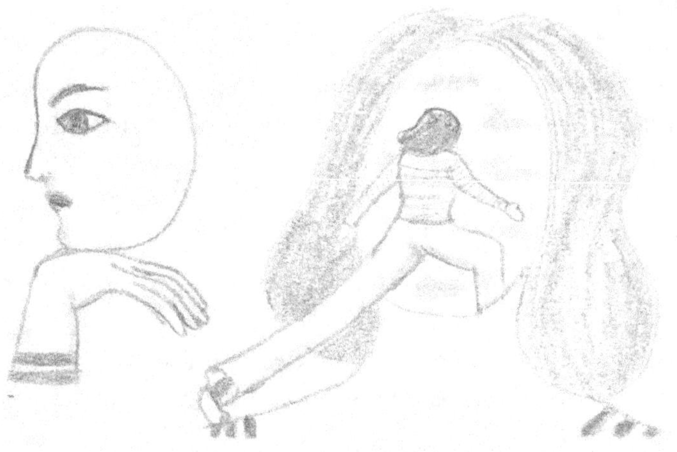

Front:

Concept: Existential Psychology
Key Figure: Rollo May
Era: 1950s
Essence: Human existence, freedom, and the quest for

meaning.

Core Ideas:Focuses on individual experience, existential anxiety, and the human condition.

Emphasizes personal responsibility, choice, and authentic living.

Back:

Impact:Transformed psychotherapeutic practices with a focus on existential dilemmas.

Inspired personal and cultural reflections on life's meaning.

Influenced educational philosophies to foster holistic development.

Critiques:Challenges in empirical testing due to abstract concepts.

Integration with other approaches for a more comprehensive understanding.

Simple Definition of Existential Psychology

Existential Psychology, spearheaded by Rollo May in the 1950s, delves into the depths of human existence, emphasizing the centrality of the human experience, freedom, and the quest for meaning. This approach contrasts with deterministic views, proposing that individuals have the capacity for self-awareness, choice, and creating values in the face of life's inherent anxieties and ambiguities (May, 1953).

Expanded Definition of Existential Psychology

At its heart, Existential Psychology posits that anxiety and conflict are inevitable parts of the human condition, arising from our confrontation with existential givens such as death, freedom, isolation, and meaninglessness. May's work underscores the importance of confronting these existential challenges to achieve authentic living and self-realization. He introduces the concept of "the courage to be," suggesting that facing life's existential dilemmas is essential for psychological growth and well-being (May, 1958).

Application of Existential Psychology

Therapeutic Practice: Existential psychology profoundly impacts psychotherapy by providing a framework that emphasizes the individual's experience of existence, freedom, and the quest for meaning. Therapists utilize existential principles to help clients face existential anxieties—such as those related to death, freedom, isolation, and meaninglessness—and to navigate the process of self-discovery and personal growth (May, 1967). This approach encourages clients to confront their life's dilemmas and to live authentically despite the inherent uncertainties of the human condition (Yalom, 1980).

Personal and Cultural Reflection: May's existential psychology prompts individuals and societies to examine the underlying values and meanings that shape their existence. It fosters a critical reflection on how existential crises can catalyze personal development and highlights the importance of establishing meaningful connections amidst modernity's dislocations (May, 1975). This perspective is particularly relevant in times of social and cultural upheaval, offering insights into how existential concerns drive collective and individual behavior (Frankl, 1946).

Educational Philosophies: Drawing from existential psychology, educational philosophies have been inspired to promote teaching methods that emphasize critical thinking, self-exploration, and the development of authentic values. Such pedagogies aim to nurture the whole person, fostering not only intellectual growth but also emotional and ethical maturity. This educational approach aligns with May's belief in the importance of confronting existential realities to achieve a fuller, more meaningful life (May, 1983).

Critiques and Adjustments:

While the existential approach offers deep insights into the human psyche, it has been critiqued for its potential abstraction and difficulty in empirical measurement. Critics argue that focusing intensely on individual subjective experiences may sideline the influences of social, cultural, and biological factors in shaping behavior and mental health (Yalom, 1980). In response, modern existential therapists often integrate existential concepts with other therapeutic modalities, such as cognitive-behavioral therapy, to address this critique, creating a more holistic approach to mental health that considers both existential dilemmas and the practical aspects of psychological well-being (Hoffman et al., 2009).

Biography

Rollo May's journey through existential psychology was not just an academic endeavor but a deeply personal exploration of what it means to be human. His writings, rich with philosophical insight, continue to resonate with those who grapple with life's existential questions. Reflecting on May's legacy, I am reminded of the enduring relevance of existential psychology in today's world—a testament to the timeless quest for meaning and authenticity in the human experience.

Structuralism

Dr. Wilhelm Wundt, PhD (1870s)

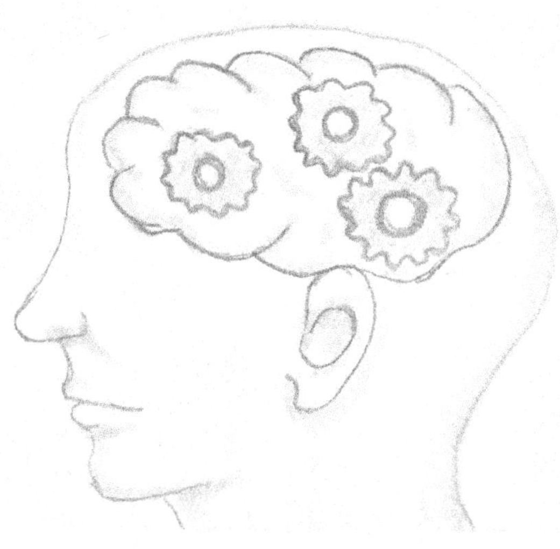

Front

Structuralism Definition: Analysis of mind's elements (thoughts, sensations, perceptions) to understand overall experience.

Originator: Wilhelm Wundt (1870s), first psychology laboratory in Leipzig, 1879.

Analogy:

Recipe Ingredients = Mind's Elements

Orchestra Instruments = Individual Mental Processes

Jigsaw Puzzle Pieces = Sensations, Thoughts, Emotions

Alphabet Letters = Components of Mental Experience

Method: Introspection - examining your own conscious experience.

Goal: Understand structure of mind by dissecting its components.

Back

Critiques: Reliance on subjective introspection.

Overemphasis on individual elements, ignoring interactions.

Historical Context:

Era of Industrial Revolution.

Movement from philosophy to scientific inquiry in psychology.

Wundt's Contribution: Pioneered scientific approach to psychology. Explored universality of mental processes. Influenced future psychological theories, despite Structuralism's limitations.

Related Contemporary: Émile Durkheim - quantifying human experiences in social sciences.

Significance: Laid groundwork for future psychological research, emphasizing scientific methods.

Structuralism: The Foundation of Psychological Inquiry

At its most basic, Structuralism in psychology is like dissecting a recipe to understand a dish. Just as a recipe is made up of individual ingredients that come together to create a specific flavor, Structuralism looks at the individual elements of the mind – such as thoughts, sensations, and perceptions – to understand the overall experience of the mind.

Structuralism, as pioneered by Wilhelm Wundt in the 1870s, marked the beginning of psychology as a distinct scientific discipline. At its core, Structuralism aimed to dissect and understand the structure of the mind by analyzing its individual components. Think of it as an attempt to understand a building by studying each brick, each window, and each door – only in this case, the building is the human mind.

To explain Structuralism in plain language, imagine looking at a red balloon. Structuralism isn't just about seeing the balloon as a whole; it's about examining every aspect of that experience – the redness of the balloon, its round shape, the feelings it evokes, and the memories it may stir. It's an effort to break down the mental processes into their simplest elements.

Examples of Structuralism

The Orchestra Metaphor: Consider an orchestra. Structuralism is akin to understanding the symphony not just as a harmonious whole but by dissecting each instrument's contribution – the violin's melody, the drum's rhythm, and the flute's timbre. It's an exploration of how these individual parts come together to create the experience of music.

A Jigsaw Puzzle: Imagine a jigsaw puzzle. Each piece is a separate entity, yet when pieced together, they form a complete picture. Structuralism attempts to understand the mind by examining each 'piece' – every sensation, thought, and emotion – and how they collectively form the human experience.

The Mosaic Example: Think of the mind as a mosaic. Each tiny tile in a mosaic is akin to a single mental process, like a thought or a sensation. Structuralism is about examining each of these tiny tiles to see how they collectively form the larger, complex picture of human consciousness. Just as you can't grasp the beauty of the mosaic without understanding its individual tiles, you can't understand the mind without looking at its individual components.

The Alphabet Analogy: Imagine the mind like an alphabet. Each letter represents a different component of our mental experience – sight, sound, emotion, etc. Structuralism aims to understand how these 'letters' combine to form 'words' (complex thoughts) and 'sentences' (stream of consciousness). Just as letters are fundamental to creating meaning in language, these basic mental elements are essential to forming the human experience.

Critiques of Structuralism

However, Structuralism was not without its critiques. One major criticism was its reliance on introspection, a method considered highly subjective. Critics argued that self-analysis could not be reliably used to establish universal truths about the human mind. Furthermore, Structuralism's focus on the individual components of the mind often overlooked the importance of how these components interacted.

Wilhelm Wundt: The Man Behind the Theory

Wilhelm Wundt, often credited as the father of modern psychology, was a figure of his time, emerging during an era marked by the Industrial Revolution. This period was characterized by a fervent desire to understand and quantify everything, extending even to the realm of the human experience. Wundt's establishment of the first psychology laboratory in 1879 at the University of Leipzig was a groundbreaking moment, symbolizing the transition of psychological study from philosophical speculation to scientific inquiry (Boring, 1950).

Wundt's primary inquiry revolved around whether the mind has a structure and whether our thoughts and mental processes are universally similar. He strived to apply rigorous scientific methods to explore these questions, a novel approach at the time. His work coincided with efforts by contemporaries like Émile Durkheim, who sought to quantify human experiences and develop methodologies for social sciences research (Durkheim, 1897).

While Wundt is celebrated for his pioneering role, it's essential to recognize that he was, in many ways, a product of his time – benefiting from being the first to formalize psychology as a science. His inquiries into the structure of the mind laid the groundwork for future psychological theories, despite the limitations and critiques of Structuralism.

In understanding Wundt and Structuralism, it's crucial to appreciate the historical and intellectual context of the era. Wundt's work was a response to the intellectual currents of his time, seeking to bring clarity and scientific rigor to the study of the human mind.

Memory and Personality

Dr. Elizabeth Loftus, PhD (1970s)

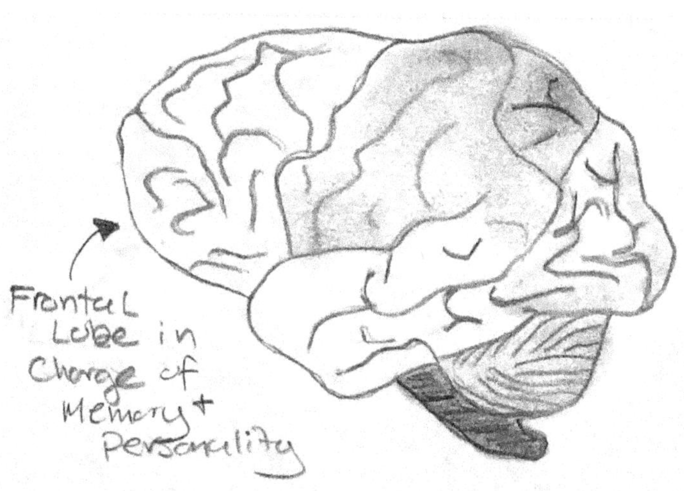

Front:

Concept: Memory Researchc

Focus: Malleability and reliability of human memory.

Key Insights: Memories are dynamic and can be influenced or altered by external factors.

Core Ideas: Memories are susceptible to distortion and the creation of false memories.

The "misinformation effect" demonstrates how post-event information can alter memory accuracy.

Back:

Impact:Legal System: Challenges the reliability of eyewitness testimony, advocating for cautious interpretation.

Psychotherapy: Influences therapeutic practices by highlighting risks of implanting false memories.

Personal Identity: Prompts reflection on how memory shapes our self-perception and personal narratives.

Critiques:Ethical concerns regarding the potential to undermine genuine experiences of trauma.

Calls for a nuanced approach to understanding memory's complexities.

Simple Definition of Memory Research

The study of memory within cognitive psychology explores the malleability and reliability of human memory, revealing how memories can be influenced, altered, or even falsely created by external factors. This line of inquiry highlights the dynamic nature of memory, challenging the notion of memories as fixed and unchangeable records of past experiences.

Expanded Definition and Key Concepts

Central to the field of memory research is the understanding that memories are susceptible to distortion through misinformation, suggestive questioning, and the misattribution of memory sources. Key findings include the "misinformation effect," where individuals' recollections of events become less accurate due to the incorporation of misleading information presented after the event. This body of work also delves into the phenomenon of false memories, showing that people can come to believe in and vividly recall events that never actually occurred, especially when exposed to suggestive cues or pressure (Loftus & Palmer, 1974; Loftus & Pickrell, 1995).

Application of Memory Research

Legal System and Eyewitness Testimony: Loftus's research has had a significant impact on the legal system, particularly regarding the reliability of eyewitness testimony. Her findings have led to changes in how eyewitness evidence is evaluated and used in courtrooms, emphasizing the need for caution in handling eyewitness accounts and the potential for memory distortion (Loftus, 1975; Loftus & Palmer, 1974).

Psychotherapy and False Memories: The implications of false memory research extend to psychotherapy, where suggestive therapeutic techniques can inadvertently create false memories of traumatic events. Loftus's work has sparked debates on the practices and ethics of recovering memories in therapy sessions, underscoring the necessity for evidence-based approaches to avoid the risk of implanting false memories (Loftus & Pickrell, 1995).

Understanding Personality: The malleability of memory also offers insights into personality development and the narrative construction of the self. Memories, including false ones, can influence an individual's self-perception, attitudes, and behaviors, suggesting that our personalities may be partly shaped by how we remember and interpret past events (Loftus, 2003).

Critiques and Contemporary Views

While Loftus's contributions to psychology are widely recognized, her work has also faced critiques, particularly from those concerned about the implications of false memory research for survivors of trauma. Critics argue that the emphasis on false memories could undermine the credibility of genuine accounts of traumatic experiences. Loftus maintains that her aim is to illuminate the workings of memory, not to invalidate personal experiences (Loftus, 1993).

Biography and Personal Reflection

The contributions of Dr. Elizabeth Loftus to our understanding of memory's malleability can't be overstated or simplified into merely 'good' or 'bad.' Reflecting on the era of the satanic panic and other memory controversies, it's evident that Loftus's work has seeped into the fabric of our collective consciousness, altering the very lexicon of how we discuss memory (Loftus, 1993). Her research has resonated through society, shedding light on the complexities of human memory and its implications for justice, personal identity, and our grasp of reality.

As someone deeply engrossed in graduate research on eyewitness identification, I've grappled with the paradoxes Loftus unveils. The fragility and suggestibility of memory, as she's demonstrated, challenge foundational assumptions about our perceptions and recollections (Loftus & Palmer, 1974). This realization is a double-edged sword. On one hand, it's a critical lens through which to scrutinize the reliability of eyewitness testimony—a cornerstone of legal proceedings that's far more precarious than previously acknowledged (Loftus, 1975).

Yet, there's a broader, more existential dimension to Loftus's work that strikes a chord with me. If our memories, and thus our identities, are so easily influenced and altered, what does that say about the essence of self? Loftus's exploration into false memories and the construction of nonexistent events (Loftus & Pickrell, 1995) beckons us to question the fabric of our personal narratives. It's a jarring reminder that the stories we tell ourselves about who we are might be as fluid as the memories they're built upon.

This contemplation leads to a profound reckoning with the nature of consciousness and selfhood. Are we, as beings, merely the sum of our memories? And if those memories can be so readily distorted, what does that make us? Loftus's research doesn't just challenge the legal system; it challenges the very notion of human integrity and authenticity (Loftus, 2003).

Elizabeth Loftus, through her meticulous and sometimes controversial work, has not only pioneered the field of memory studies but has also compelled us to confront uncomfortable truths about our malleability and vulnerability. As someone who has navigated the treacherous waters of memory in academic research, I find Loftus's contributions both illuminating and disconcerting. They serve as a constant reminder of the power of memory, not just in shaping our past but in constructing our reality and our future.

16PF

Dr. Raymond Cattell, PhD (1940s)

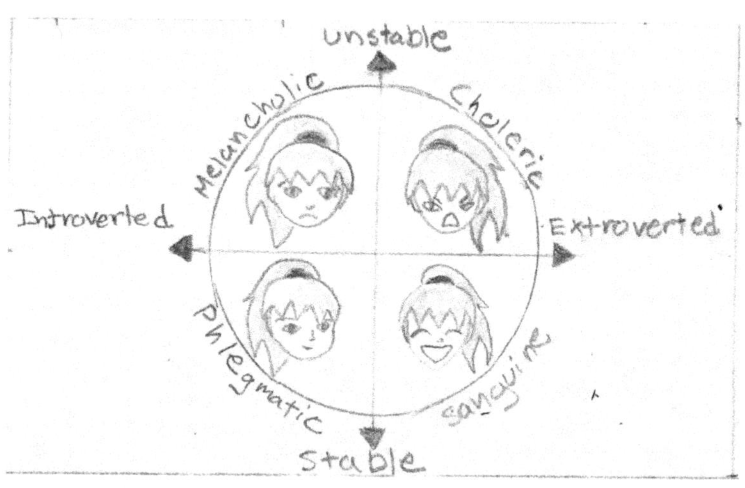

Front:

   Concept: 16 Personality Factors (16PF)

   Era: 1940s

   Key Figure: Raymond Cattell

   Essence: Comprehensive tool for assessing personality traits.

   Core Ideas:Identifies sixteen primary traits that constitute human personality.

   Utilizes factor analysis to understand personality structure.

Back:

   Impact: Clinical Psychology: Aids in diagnosis and treatment planning.

   Organizational Psychology: Enhances personnel selection and leadership development.

   Academic Research: Supports studies on personality and behavior correlations.

   Critiques: Faces critiques regarding its factor structure compared to simpler models like the Five Factor Model.

   Advocates highlight its detailed trait analysis for nuanced personality assessment.

Simple Definition of the 16PF

The 16 Personality Factors (16PF) questionnaire, developed by Raymond Cattell in the 1940s, represents a comprehensive tool for assessing the broad spectrum of human personality. Based on factor analysis, the 16PF identifies sixteen primary traits that Cattell theorized to constitute the building blocks of individual personality. This assessment provides insights into personality structure, offering a quantitative basis for understanding behavioral tendencies (Cattell, 1946).

Expanded Definition and Key Concepts

Cattell's approach to personality psychology was grounded in the empirical analysis of trait taxonomy. Through extensive data collection and statistical methods, he distilled personality into sixteen distinct factors, ranging from warmth and reasoning to apprehension and openness to change. Each factor is scored on a continuum, with the 16PF yielding profiles that depict an individual's unique blend of traits (Cattell, Eber, & Tatsuoka, 1970).

Application of the 16PF

Clinical Psychology: The 16PF questionnaire is utilized in clinical settings to aid in diagnosis, treatment planning, and understanding patients' personality structures. It helps clinicians identify psychological conditions, predict therapeutic outcomes, and tailor interventions to suit individual personality profiles (Cattell & Mead, 2008).

Organizational Psychology: In the realm of organizational psychology, the 16PF is applied in personnel selection, leadership development, and team-building exercises. By assessing key personality traits, organizations can make informed decisions about hiring, promoting, and developing employees to enhance workplace dynamics and productivity (Russell & Karol, 2002).

Research and Academia: Cattell's 16PF has also served as a foundational tool for academic research, contributing to the broader understanding of personality and its impact on various life outcomes. Studies utilizing the 16PF have explored correlations between personality traits and behaviors, such as job performance, academic achievement, and interpersonal relationships (Cattell & Krug, 1986).

Critiques and Contemporary Views

While the 16PF has been a valuable instrument in personality psychology, it has faced critiques related to its factor structure and the relevance of some traits in contemporary models of personality. Critics argue that subsequent models, like the Five Factor Model (FFM), offer a more parsimonious representation of personality. However, proponents of the 16PF assert that its comprehensive trait coverage provides a nuanced understanding of personality beyond the scope of the FFM (McCrae & Costa, 1987).

Raymond Cattell's pioneering work in personality assessment and his development of the 16PF have left an indelible mark on the field of psychology. His commitment to empirical research and statistical analysis reshaped how personality is conceptualized and measured. Reflecting on Cattell's contributions, it's clear that his legacy endures in the continued use of the 16PF in various settings, underscoring the complexity and diversity of human personality.

Note on the Inclusion of the "Intelligence"

The inclusion of a chapter on intelligence in a book primarily focused on theories of personality might initially seem unconventional. However, the decision to explore intelligence alongside personality theories is deliberate and reflects a broader, more integrative understanding of human behavior and cognition.

Intelligence and personality are deeply intertwined aspects of the human psyche, each influencing how individuals navigate the world, solve problems, interact with others, and understand themselves. While personality theories delve into the patterns of thoughts, feelings, and behaviors that make each person unique, intelligence offers insight into the cognitive capacities that underlie these patterns. Together, they provide a more comprehensive view of the individual.

Alfred Binet's work, central to this chapter, underscores the adaptive nature of intelligence, aligning closely with personality psychology's concerns. Binet's emphasis on mental agility and the capacity to learn and adapt to new situations echoes the adaptability and growth aspects often explored in personality theories. Moreover, understanding the historical and conceptual roots of intelligence assessment illuminates how perceptions of cognitive abilities have shaped, and been shaped by, broader societal understandings of human potential and individual differences.

This chapter aims to bridge the conceptual gap between intelligence and personality, highlighting the interplay between cognitive abilities and personality traits. It underscores the importance of a nuanced approach to understanding the full spectrum of human psychology, beyond the traditional boundaries of separate constructs. By including intelligence in this discussion, we invite readers to consider the multifaceted nature of human cognition and behavior and the myriad ways in which intelligence and personality interact to shape our lives.

In essence, the chapter on intelligence enriches the conversation on personality theories by providing a critical perspective on how cognitive functions contribute to the complex tapestry of human nature. It encourages a holistic view of psychological science, where the exploration of intelligence complements and deepens our understanding of personality and the diverse ways individuals experience and engage with the world.Exploring the Concept of Intelligence

Intelligence

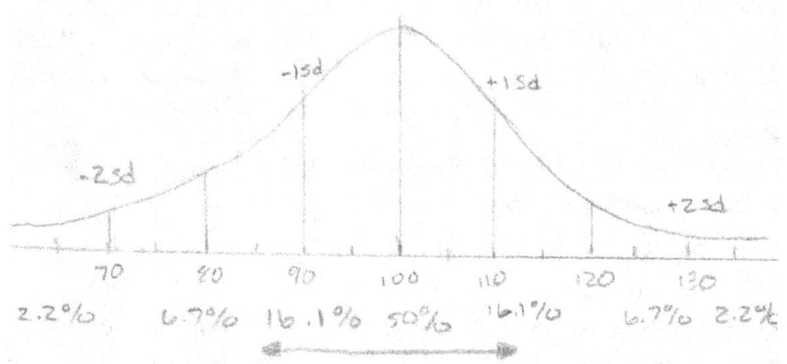

Front:

Focus: Interplay between cognitive abilities and personality.

Key Concepts:

Cognitive Abilities

Problem-Solving

Learning & Adaptation

Back:

Alfred Binet's Contribution:

Developed the first intelligence test, laying the groundwork for future assessments.

Modern Assessments: Evolution from the Binet-Simon scale to contemporary IQ tests and beyond.

Significance: Intelligence plays a crucial role in personal growth, educational strategies, and understanding human potential.

Insight: Intelligence and personality together offer a comprehensive view of human behavior, emphasizing the multifaceted nature of psychological assessment.

Intelligence remains one of the most intriguing and debated constructs in psychology. It encompasses a range of cognitive abilities, including problem-solving, learning, reasoning, and understanding complex ideas. Intelligence is not just about knowledge but about the capacity to apply knowledge adaptively in various situations (Sternberg, 1999).

Alfred Binet's Pioneering Contribution

Alfred Binet, a French psychologist, significantly shaped the early understanding of intelligence. In collaboration with

Theodore Simon, Binet developed the first practical intelligence test in the early 20th century. Their work was motivated by the need to identify schoolchildren who required special educational interventions. The Binet-Simon scale introduced innovative concepts such as mental age, offering a nuanced view of intellectual development (Binet & Simon, 1905).

From Binet to Modern Assessments

Binet's foundational work laid the groundwork for future intelligence testing. His concept of mental age was further developed into the intelligence quotient (IQ) by William Stern, leading to the Stanford-Binet Intelligence Scale's creation by Lewis Terman. This evolution marked the beginning of standardized intelligence testing, which has since expanded to include various models and assessments, such as the Wechsler Adult Intelligence Scale (WAIS) and the Wechsler Intelligence Scale for Children (WISC) (Wechsler, 1955).

Intelligence as Adaptation

A core aspect of intelligence, as viewed by Binet and later theorists, is its role in adaptation to the environment. This view posits that intelligence reflects an individual's ability to modify their behavior in response to new information or challenges, underscoring the dynamic interplay between cognitive abilities and the environment (Sternberg & Detterman, 1986).

Multiple Intelligences and Beyond

The study of intelligence has evolved to recognize its multifaceted nature. Howard Gardner's theory of multiple intelligences, for example, suggests that intelligence encompasses a broad range of cognitive abilities, from linguistic and logical-mathematical to musical and interpersonal intelligences, challenging the traditional IQ-based view of intelligence (Gardner, 1983).

Contemporary Perspectives and Challenges

Today, the study of intelligence continues to evolve, integrating insights from neuroscience, psychology, and education. Researchers explore the genetic and environmental influences on intelligence, the role of working memory and processing speed, and the impact of educational interventions on cognitive development. Despite advances, the assessment and interpretation of intelligence remain complex, with ongoing debates about the roles of culture, equity, and bias in intelligence testing (Nisbett et al., 2012).

Personal Construct Psychology

Dr. George Kelly, PhD (1950s)

Front:

Concept: Personal Construct Psychology

Focus: How individuals use personal constructs to interpret experiences.

Key Insight: Reality is constructed through individual lenses of understanding.

Core Ideas: Personal constructs are bipolar dimensions used to categorize experiences.

Emphasizes the fluidity and adaptability of personal constructs over time.

Back:

Impact:Psychotherapy: Aids in exploring clients' worldviews for tailored interventions.

Organizational Behavior: Enhances understanding of workplace dynamics.

Educational Psychology: Informs strategies for engaging and effective learning.

Initial Take: Initially seems like an intuitive understanding of self-construction, yet promises deeper, nuanced insights upon closer examination.

Simple Definition of Personal Construct Psychology

Personal Construct Psychology (PCP) is a theory that views individuals as active participants in shaping their perceptions of the world. According to this perspective, people use personal constructs, which are bipolar dimensions of judgment, to categorize their experiences and anticipate future events. This approach emphasizes the subjective nature of cognition and suggests that our understanding and behavior are guided by how we predict and interpret our surroundings.

Expanded Definition and Key Concepts

Central to PCP is the notion that personal realities are constructed through individual systems of personal constructs. These constructs serve as the lenses through which experiences are interpreted, enabling individuals to navigate life's challenges and opportunities. The theory posits that personal constructs are flexible and can be reevaluated and changed in light of new experiences, highlighting the dynamic nature of human cognition and the capacity for growth and adaptation.

Application of Personal Construct Psychology

Clinical Psychology: PCP has profoundly influenced therapeutic practices by providing a framework for understanding clients' viewpoints and the constructs they use to perceive their problems. Techniques such as the Repertory Grid Technique allow clinicians to explore and map an individual's personal constructs, facilitating more personalized and effective interventions (Kelly, 1955; Fransella, Bell, & Bannister, 2004).

Organizational Development: In organizational settings, PCP offers insights into how employees' personal constructs influence their behavior and interactions at work. Understanding these constructs can aid in conflict resolution, leadership development, and team dynamics, promoting a more cohesive and productive workplace environment (Neimeyer & Neimeyer, 2003).

Educational Psychology: Kelly's theory has applications in educational psychology, particularly in understanding how students' personal constructs affect their learning and motivation. By recognizing and addressing the individual constructs students bring to the classroom, educators can tailor their teaching strategies to better meet students' needs and foster a more engaging learning experience (Ravenette, 1998).

Critiques and Contemporary Views

While PCP has been lauded for its innovative approach to understanding human psychology, it has also faced critiques regarding its abstract nature and the challenge of operationalizing personal constructs for empirical research. Critics argue that the subjective nature of personal constructs can complicate the measurement and validation of the theory's constructs (Neimeyer, 1985).

Biography and Personal Reflection

Personal Construct Psychology is one of those realms I've marked for a deeper dive, though I confess it initially struck me as another entry in the vast ocean of psychological theories preaching the gospel of finding meaning within oneself. At first glance, it feels a bit like grabbing at low-hanging fruit—this idea that we construct our realities through personal lenses is, on the surface, a "well, of course" moment (Kelly, 1955).

There's an inherent appeal in theories that validate our inner experiences and the frameworks we use to navigate life. Yet, I can't shake a certain apprehension towards what sometimes feels like an oversimplification of the complex tapestry of human cognition and behavior. It's not that I find the concept unimportant—far from it. The notion that our personal constructs shape our interpretation of the world is both fascinating and undeniably logical. It's just that the initial simplicity masks a deeper, more nuanced investigation into how we perceive, interact with, and ultimately create our existential realities (Kelly, 1955).

As someone who doesn't claim expertise in this particular corner of psychology, my initial skepticism might stem from a superficial understanding of Kelly's work. The more I learn, the more I appreciate the theory's depth and its potential applications, from psychotherapy to organizational development (Neimeyer & Neimeyer, 2003; Fransella, Bell, & Bannister, 2004). There's a richness in the idea that by examining and potentially restructuring our personal constructs, we can alter our perceptions and interactions with the world around us.

So, while my first impression was a mix of intrigue and skepticism, I'm open to the possibility that a deeper engagement with Personal Construct Psychology might reveal insights that are anything but obvious. It's a reminder that the initial simplicity of many psychological theories often belies a complexity that merits a closer look. As I delve further into Kelly's theory and its broader implications, I'll be looking for those moments of revelation that challenge my initial apprehensions.

In preparing for a more informed critique or endorsement in a future edition, I acknowledge the gap in my understanding and the journey ahead in exploring the intricacies of how we construct our psychological landscapes. Perhaps, in this exploration, I'll find that what appeared as low-hanging fruit offers a taste of something far more substantive and nourishing for thought (Kelly, 1955).

Locus of Control

Dr. Julian Rotter, PhD (1950s)

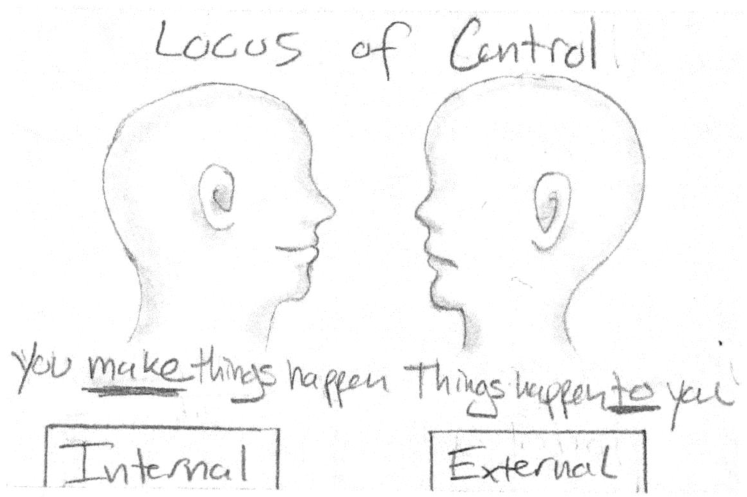

Front:

Concept: Locus of Control

Focus: Impact of internal vs. external beliefs on life.

Philosophical Echoes: Reflects stoic principles on control and acceptance.

Back:

Insight: Ties to Jungian psychology and modern self-help philosophies.

Explores the balance between accepting fate and asserting control.

Impact: Influences personal development and therapeutic practices.

Encourages a reflective approach to personal and external challenges.

Reflection: Serves as a foundational concept in understanding personal agency.

Bridges psychology and philosophy, offering a nuanced view of human behavior.

Simple Definition of Locus of Control

Locus of Control refers to the degree to which individuals believe they have control over the outcomes of events in their lives. It distinguishes between two orientations: an internal locus of control, where individuals attribute their successes or failures to their own actions, and an external locus of control, where people believe that external forces or chance determine their outcomes.

Expanded Definition and Key Concepts

This concept plays a crucial role in understanding human behavior and motivation, suggesting that an individual's locus of control orientation can significantly influence their approach to life's challenges and opportunities. Those with an internal locus of control tend to perceive themselves as the architects of their fate, likely to take initiative and persist in overcoming obstacles. In contrast, individuals with an external locus of control may feel that their efforts have little impact on their lives, which can affect their motivation and resilience.

Application of Locus of Control

Clinical Psychology: In therapeutic contexts, understanding a client's locus of control orientation is crucial for tailoring treatment approaches. Clinicians often work to shift an overly external locus of control towards a more balanced or internal orientation, aiming to enhance the client's sense of agency and efficacy. Techniques might include cognitive-behavioral strategies that challenge external attributions of control and reinforce the client's capacity to effect change in their life (Rotter, 1975). This shift can be particularly beneficial in treating conditions like depression and anxiety, where feelings of helplessness and lack of control are prevalent.

Educational Settings: The concept of locus of control has significant implications for education, where fostering an internal locus of control among students is associated with higher academic motivation and achievement. Educators can implement strategies that promote autonomy, provide constructive feedback, and emphasize the role of effort in success to support the development of an internal locus of control (Rotter, 1982). Recognizing and addressing external control beliefs can also help identify students who may benefit from targeted interventions to improve their academic engagement and performance.

Organizational Behavior: In the workplace, employees with an internal locus of control are often more proactive, take initiative, and exhibit higher levels of job satisfaction and performance. Managers can encourage an internal locus of control by creating an empowering work environment that provides employees with opportunities for decision-making and recognizes their contributions to organizational success (Rotter, 1975). Additionally, understanding the locus of control orientation can aid in leadership development, team-building, and conflict resolution by aligning tasks and roles with individuals' perceptions of control.

Health and Well-being: Locus of control impacts individuals' health behaviors and attitudes. Those with an internal locus of control are more likely to engage in health-promoting behaviors, believe in the efficacy of taking proactive health measures, and adhere to treatment recommendations. Public health interventions and educational campaigns can leverage these insights to design programs that enhance individuals' sense of control over their health outcomes (Rotter, 1975).

Contemporary Research and Adjustments:

Recent research has sought to refine the locus of control

concept by exploring its nuances, including the spectrum of control beliefs and the context-dependent nature of these beliefs. Modern approaches often integrate locus of control with other psychological constructs, such as self-efficacy and resilience, to provide a more comprehensive understanding of how control beliefs influence behavior and psychological well-being.

By delving into the wide-ranging applications of Locus of Control and acknowledging ongoing research in the field, this expanded discussion highlights the profound impact of control beliefs on various domains of human life, emphasizing the value of fostering a balanced locus of control for enhancing personal and collective outcomes.

Locus of Control: Between Philosophy and Psychology

Whenever I dive into discussions about Locus of Control, my mind inevitably drifts back to Carl Jung. That connection might seem a bit left-field, but it's deeply rooted in how I was introduced to psychological concepts. Locus of Control emerged in my research as a pivotal idea, one that seems to have infiltrated modern self-help literature. You know the type— those "Don't sweat the small stuff" and "Let it slide" mantras that champion the essence of external locus control versus the internal drive to master one's fate (Rotter, 1954).

At its core, Locus of Control circles back to the age-old philosophical debates about the power of internal versus external forces in shaping our lives. It's fascinating how this psychological concept mirrors the discussions you'd find in a dialectical behavior therapy session or in the musings of a personality theory class. These explorations often tread the fine line between being theories of personality and full-blown philosophical doctrines.

In essence, Locus of Control served as my gateway into understanding the dynamic interplay between internal and external influences. It's a concept that, for me, ties closely with the stoic wisdom of Marcus Aurelius—there's a certain stoicism to recognizing what aspects of life we can control and what we must let go (Rotter, 1966). This recognition lays down a foundation for navigating life's complexities, not just in the realm of personal development but across the spectrum of human experience.

The more I reflect on it, the more Locus of Control resonates with me as more than just a psychological construct. It's a lens through which we can view our approach to life's challenges and our pursuit of personal growth. The idea that we might be at the mercy of external forces or, conversely, that we hold the reins to our destiny, is a powerful realization that influences not just our actions but our perceptions of self and the world around us.

This blend of psychology and philosophy, encapsulated in the concept of Locus of Control, underscores much of what draws me to the study of the human mind and behavior. It's a reminder of the depth and breadth of psychology—not just as a field of study but as a reflection of the human condition. As I continue to explore the nuances of Locus of Control and its applications, I'm reminded of its relevance not only in academic discourse but in the practical wisdom it offers for leading a balanced and reflective life.

By weaving together the psychological underpinnings of Locus of Control with philosophical reflections, this personal reflection captures your engagement with the concept and its significance both within and beyond the realm of psychology.

Obedience to Authority

Dr. Stanley Milgram, PhD (1960s)

Front:

Concept: Obedience to Authority

Theorist: Dr. Stanley Milgram, PhD

Decade: 1960s

Key Idea: Investigates why individuals comply with authority, even against personal ethics.

Milgram's Experiment: Demonstrated the extent to which people are willing to follow orders from an authority figure, even to the point of causing harm to others.

Back:

Findings: A significant majority of participants were prepared to administer electric shocks to a stranger when instructed by an authority figure.

Applications: Highlights the impact of authority on human behavior, informing practices in education, military, and organizational behavior.

Critiques: Ethical concerns about participant distress led to changes in research ethics guidelines.

Legacy: Milgram's work remains a cornerstone in social psychology, illustrating the powerful influence of authority on obedience and contributing to our understanding of social dynamics.

Simple Definition of Obedience to Authority

Obedience to authority describes the tendency of individuals to comply with instructions from authority figures, even when such compliance conflicts with their personal morals or ethical standards (Milgram, 1963).

Expanded Definition and Context

In the early 1960s, Stanley Milgram conducted a series of experiments to explore the limits of human obedience to authority, motivated by the atrocities of World War II and the subsequent Nuremberg Trials. Milgram's research sought to understand how ordinary people could be compelled to commit acts that violated their ethical principles under authoritative pressure (Milgram, 1963).

Milgram's Experiment

Milgram (1963) devised a scenario where participants were led to believe they were administering electric shocks to another person as part of a learning experiment. Despite the "learner" expressing pain and discomfort, participants continued to administer shocks when prompted by an authority figure, revealing a startling level of obedience.

Findings and Implications

The results, showing a high degree of compliance with the authority's commands to inflict pain, challenged previous beliefs about the nature of obedience and moral integrity (Milgram, 1963). Milgram's work illuminated the powerful influence of authority on behavior and sparked significant ethical debates and research in social psychology.

Real-World Applications

Understanding Compliance: Milgram's findings have profound

implications for understanding behavior in hierarchical organizations, such as the military and workplaces, highlighting the need for ethical leadership (Milgram, 1963).

Educational Practices: The experiments underscore the importance of teaching critical thinking and moral reasoning to resist unethical authority pressures (Milgram, 1963).

Critiques and Ethical Considerations

Milgram's experiments faced criticism for ethical concerns, particularly the emotional distress experienced by participants. This criticism led to stricter ethical guidelines in psychological research (Baumrind, 1964).

Legacy of Stanley Milgram.

I've harbored a profound admiration for Stanley Milgram's experiments for as long as I can remember. Their striking revelations and the boldness of Milgram's approach captured my attention early in my academic journey. It's no minor detail that a poster of the obedience to authority apparatus has adorned the walls of my office and apartment at various points in my life. This visual homage speaks volumes about the impact Milgram's work has had on me, serving as a constant reminder of the depth and complexity of human behavior under authority (Milgram, 1963).

Beyond the famed obedience studies, Milgram's innovative spirit ventured into the realms of social networks with his "small-world" experiment, laying the groundwork for what we now refer to as the "six degrees of separation" concept (Milgram,

1967). This notion, popularized in the game "Six Degrees of Kevin Bacon," owes its existence to Milgram's curiosity and scientific rigor, demonstrating his far-reaching influence beyond the confines of obedience research.

Stanley Milgram was, without a doubt, a pioneering figure whose contributions extended well beyond his most controversial work. While I hold his experiments in high esteem, it's crucial to approach his legacy with a balanced perspective. Milgram's research, particularly the obedience experiments, sparked a necessary discourse on ethical standards in psychological research, highlighting the fine line between scientific exploration and the welfare of participants (Baumrind, 1964).

In reflecting on Milgram's body of work, my admiration is tinged with a critical awareness of the ethical considerations his experiments raised. Despite these critiques, Milgram's contributions to our understanding of human behavior, social networks, and the power dynamics of authority and obedience remain unparalleled. His work continues to fascinate, provoke thought, and inspire debate among psychologists, underscoring his lasting legacy as a groundbreaking scientist whose research transcended the academic sphere and permeated popular culture.

Social Development Theory

Dr. Lev Vygotsky, PhD (1930s)

Front:

Concept: Social Development Theory

Originator: Lev Vygotsky (1930s)

Essence: Cognitive development through social interaction.

Core Concepts:Zone of Proximal Development (ZPD)

Scaffolding More Knowledgeable Other (MKO)

Back:

ZPD: Gap between what a learner can do alone and with help.

Scaffolding: Support tailored to the learner's ZPD, gradually withdrawn as independence grows.

MKO: An individual (teacher, peer) providing guidance within the ZPD.

Applications: Enhances educational practices via collaborative learning.

Integrates cultural and social contexts into child development.

Adapts special education to meet diverse learning needs.

Impact: Vygotsky's work unites cultural anthropology with cognitive psychology, offering a holistic view of development influenced by social, cultural, and individual factors.

Simple Definition of Social Development Theory

Social Development Theory, developed by Lev Vygotsky in the 1930s, posits that social interaction plays a fundamental role in the development of cognition. Vygotsky argued that community and culture profoundly influence an individual's learning process, emphasizing that cognitive development is largely a socially mediated activity.

Expanded Definition of Social Development Theory

At the core of Vygotsky's theory is the concept that the development of human understanding occurs first through social interaction and then within the individual. This perspective marks a departure from the view that cognitive development is merely a solitary endeavor. Vygotsky introduced several key concepts to articulate this theory:

Zone of Proximal Development (ZPD): Vygotsky defined the ZPD as the difference between what a learner can do without help and what they can achieve with guidance and encouragement from a skilled partner. This concept underscores the importance of scaffolding in learning, where the support is gradually withdrawn as the learner gains independence (Vygotsky, 1978).

Scaffolding: A technique based on the ZPD, where teachers or more knowledgeable peers provide structured support to learners. This support helps learners achieve tasks they cannot complete independently, facilitating their progression toward higher levels of understanding and skill.

More Knowledgeable Other (MKO): Vygotsky's term for someone who has a better understanding or a higher ability level than the learner, with respect to a particular task, process, or concept. The MKO could be a teacher, peer, or even a computer program that provides guidance.

Applications of Social Development Theory

Educational Practices: Vygotsky's theory has significantly influenced educational strategies, particularly in emphasizing collaborative learning, peer tutoring, and the tailored support of students' learning journeys. Educators are encouraged to assess each student's ZPD to provide appropriate challenges and support, promoting deeper understanding and mastery of skills.

Child Development: Understanding the social contexts of learning has led to a greater appreciation of the role of cultural tools, language, and interaction in cognitive development. This insight has informed parenting practices and early childhood education, highlighting the importance of engaging children in meaningful social activities and conversations.

Special Education: Vygotsky's work has also impacted the field of special education, where his ideas about the ZPD and scaffolding have been applied to support learners with diverse needs, ensuring that they receive the appropriate level of challenge and assistance.

Critiques and Contemporary Views

While Vygotsky's Social Development Theory has been widely embraced, some critiques focus on the difficulty of defining the ZPD's boundaries and the challenge of operationalizing scaffolding in diverse educational settings. Despite these challenges, Vygotsky's emphasis on the social and cultural dimensions of learning continues to inspire ongoing research and practice in educational psychology.

Legacy of Lev Vygotsky

Lev Vygotsky's contributions to psychology and education have left a lasting legacy, fundamentally shaping how we understand the process of learning and development. His work has bridged the gap between cultural anthropology and cognitive psychology, offering a comprehensive framework that integrates the social, cultural, and individual facets of development. Vygotsky's insights have not only advanced academic discourse but also informed practical approaches to teaching and learning, making his theories as relevant today as they were in the 1930s.

Conformity Experiments

Dr. Solomon Asch, PhD (1950s)

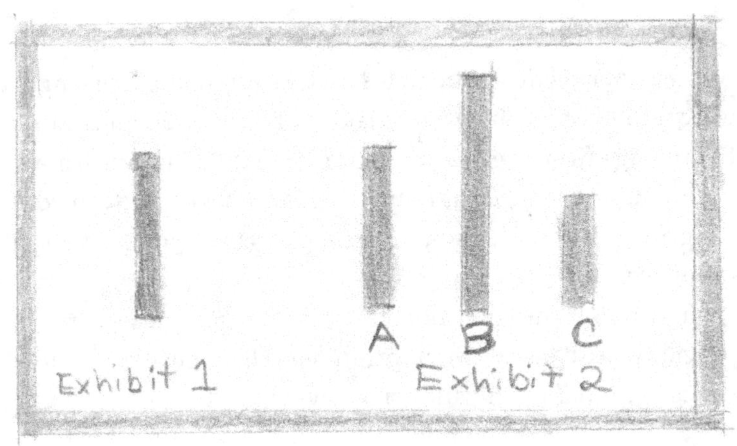

Front:

Concept: Conformity Experiments

Researcher: Dr. Solomon Asch, PhD

Era: 1950s

Focus: The influence of group pressure on individual judgment and decisions.

Relevance: Asch's work offers a critical lens on current societal phenomena like groupthink, misinformation, and political polarization, underscoring the importance of fostering independent thinking and resilience against undue social pressures.

Back:

Key Experiment: Participants asked to compare line lengths were influenced by incorrect majority answers, demonstrating the strong effect of group pressure on individual conformity.

Findings: A significant number of individuals conformed to the group's incorrect choices, highlighting the power of social influence.

Implications: Insights into how and why individuals conform provide essential understanding in fields like social psychology, education, and organizational behavior.

Simple Definition of Conformity

Conformity involves changing one's behavior or beliefs in response to explicit or implicit pressure from others (Asch, 1955).

Expanded Definition and Context

Solomon Asch's pioneering research in the 1950s sought to systematically investigate the phenomenon of conformity, demonstrating how social pressure could lead individuals to conform to an incorrect majority opinion (Asch, 1955).

Asch's Conformity Experiments

Asch's conformity experiments, conducted in the 1950s, stand as a seminal body of work in social psychology, illustrating the powerful influence of group pressure on individual judgments and behaviors. These experiments were designed to explore the extent to which social forces alter people's opinions or behaviors to conform with group norms, even when those norms are clearly incorrect.

In these studies, participants were placed in a group with others, whom they believed were fellow participants but were actually confederates of the experimenter. The task was straightforward: each member of the group had to state aloud which of three comparison lines matched a standard line in length. The correct answer was obvious, making this a test not of perception but of the willingness to conform.

Initially, the confederates gave correct answers, but eventually, they began to provide incorrect responses unanimously. The key measure was whether the true participant would conform to the group's incorrect consensus or trust their own senses and provide the correct answer.

The findings were striking. Asch found that a significant proportion of participants conformed to the group's incorrect response at least once during the trials, with the overall rate of conformity being around one-third of the responses. This result highlighted the strong influence of social pressure on conformity, suggesting that the desire for social harmony or fear of social rejection could lead individuals to conform to group norms, even when those norms are objectively wrong.

Furthermore, Asch's experiments revealed that the size of the majority, the presence of at least one ally who dissented from the majority opinion, and the public or private nature of responses influenced the level of conformity. Specifically, conformity increased with the group size up to a point but did not significantly increase beyond three to four confederates. The presence of a dissenting ally drastically reduced conformity, underscoring the power of social support in resisting group pressure. Lastly, when participants could respond privately, conformity rates dropped, indicating that much of the conformity observed was likely due to the fear of social disapproval rather than a change in personal judgment.

Asch's work has profound implications for understanding social behavior, illustrating how group dynamics can influence individual decision-making processes. It sheds light on the conditions under which people are more likely to conform and the psychological mechanisms driving conformity, offering insights into the power of social influence and the challenges of maintaining personal integrity and independence in group settings.

Findings and Implications

The results revealed a strong tendency to conform, with many subjects agreeing with the group's incorrect responses despite clear evidence to the contrary. Asch's experiments highlighted the power of social influence and the conditions under which conformity is more likely to occur (Asch, 1956).

Real-World Applications

Understanding Group Dynamics: Asch's findings are crucial for comprehending how group pressure influences individual decisions, relevant in contexts such as jury decisions, classroom settings, and corporate boardrooms (Asch, 1955).

Educational Practices: These insights underscore the importance of encouraging independent thinking and resilience against peer pressure in educational curricula (Asch, 1956).

Organizational Behavior: Knowledge of conformity mechanisms can help develop strategies to foster innovation and prevent groupthink within organizations (Asch, 1955).

Critiques and Contemporary Views

Subsequent research has explored variables affecting conformity, such as the size of the majority, the presence of dissenting opinions, and the confidence of the individual, thereby expanding on Asch's original findings (Morris & Miller, 1975).

Legacy of Solomon Asch

Solomon Asch's explorations into conformity have never felt more pertinent than they do today, in an era where misinformation thrives, and groupthink seems to dominate our collective consciousness. The digital age, with its social media echo chambers, and a political landscape deeply entrenched in partisanship, mirrors the very phenomena Asch sought to understand. His work, a beacon in the murky waters of social psychology, offers profound insights into the mechanics of societal division and consensus, making it incredibly relevant to the challenges we face in the United States and beyond.

I've always believed that understanding the forces that drive us to conform or stand apart is crucial, particularly now, as we navigate the complexities of the 21st century. The issues we encounter today—echo chambers, political divisiveness, and the overwhelming tide of public opinion—underscore the enduring significance of Asch's research on conformity. It's not about taking sides or espousing political views; it's about recognizing the fundamental dynamics of human behavior that Asch so elegantly laid bare.

In reflecting on Asch's legacy, I'm reminded of the value of his work in shedding light on our present circumstances. The division and conformity we witness today are not just echoes of the past; they are vivid illustrations of the principles Asch revealed through his experiments. His contributions go beyond academic circles, offering a lens through which we can better understand and perhaps navigate the challenges of group influence that permeate our lives.

As we stand in the early decades of this century, facing un-precedented levels of division and conformity, Asch's work remains a vital tool for understanding the undercurrents of our society. It's a testament to the power of psychological research in illuminating the paths through which individuals and societies navigate the complex web of social influence. So, here's to Dr. Solomon Asch—may his insights continue to enlighten us, offering guidance and clarity in times when the pull of the majority feels insurmountable.

NOTE: On Conformity and Obedience

While the chapters on Solomon Asch's conformity experiments and Stanley Milgram's obedience studies might initially seem out of place in a handbook predominantly focused on theories of personality, their inclusion is both deliberate and essential. These landmark studies, though not theories of personality per se, offer profound insights into the social and environmental influences on individual behavior, which in turn interact with and shape personality.

Asch's work on conformity and Milgram's investigations into obedience to authority delve into the psychological mechanisms that drive individuals to align their actions and beliefs with group norms or authoritative directives, even when doing so conflicts with their personal values or perceptions of reality. These phenomena are critical to understanding the broader context in which personality develops and operates. Specifically, they highlight the powerful role of social context, illustrating how external pressures can override individual differences in behavior and decision-making.

The relevance of these studies extends far beyond academic interest; they have real-world implications for understanding phenomena such as groupthink, radicalization, and the spread of misinformation. In today's world, where social and media influences are omnipresent and potent, Asch's and Milgram's findings are more applicable than ever. They remind us of the importance of critical thinking, the value of dissent in a healthy society, and the need for education that empowers individuals to resist undue social pressure.

By exploring the interplay between individual predispositions and social forces, these chapters enrich our understanding of personality in a holistic sense. They serve as a bridge between the study of individual traits and the broader sociocultural dynamics that influence human behavior, underscoring the complexity of the human psyche and the multifaceted nature of personality development.

Hierarchy of Needs

Dr. Abraham Maslow, PhD (1940s)

Front:

Theory: Hierarchy of Needs

Proposed by: Dr. Abraham Maslow, PhD

Foundation: Humans are motivated by a series of hierarchical needs, from basic to self-fulfillment.

The Needs: Physiological: Basic survival needs (food, water, shelter). Safety: Security and protection. Love/Belonging: Social relationships and connectedness. Esteem: Respect, self-esteem, and recognition. Self-Actualization: Achieving one's full potential and creative fulfillment.

Back:

Impact: Maslow's theory has influenced psychology, education, business, and beyond, emphasizing the importance of addressing basic needs for higher-level growth.

Critiques: Debated for its linear progression assumption and cultural universality.

Legacy: A cornerstone in understanding human motivation and development, Maslow's Hierarchy of Needs continues to be a vital framework in various fields.

Simple Definition of Hierarchy of Needs

The Hierarchy of Needs is a psychological theory proposed by Abraham Maslow, which posits that humans are motivated by a series of five basic needs arranged in a hierarchy: physiological, safety, love/belonging, esteem, and self-actualization (Maslow, 1943).

Expanded Definition and Context

Maslow's theory suggests that individuals are driven to fulfill their basic needs before moving on to higher levels of needs. The hierarchy is often depicted as a pyramid, with the most fundamental needs at the bottom and the need for self-actualization at the top.

Maslow's Hierarchy of Needs

1.Physiological Needs: These are the basic requirements for human survival, such as food, water, and shelter (Maslow, 1943).

2. Safety Needs: Once physiological needs are met, individuals seek safety and security, including personal safety, financial security, and health (Maslow, 1943).

3. Love and Belongingness Needs: Humans then strive for social relationships, including friendships, romantic attachments, and family (Maslow, 1954).

4. Esteem Needs: This level includes the need for self-esteem, respect, status, and recognition from others (Maslow, 1954).

5. Self-Actualization Needs: The highest level represents the realization of an individual's potential, self-fulfillment, and personal growth (Maslow, 1954).

Maslow's Hierarchy of Needs has had a profound impact on various fields, including psychology, education, and business. It has informed approaches to motivational strategies, human resource management, and personal development.

Critiques and Contemporary Views

Maslow's Hierarchy of Needs continues to serve as a foundational framework in psychology, offering insights into human motivation that are increasingly relevant in addressing contemporary challenges. Its applications span across various fields, illustrating its enduring impact.

Mental Health and Well-being: In an era where mental health awareness is rising, Maslow's emphasis on psychological needs and self-actualization resonates strongly. Understanding and addressing the lower levels of the hierarchy are crucial in mental health interventions, providing a roadmap for achieving higher well-being and fulfillment.

Workplace and Organizational Culture: Modern organizations increasingly focus on creating environments that fulfill employees' higher-order needs, such as esteem and self-actualization, recognizing their role in enhancing motivation, satisfaction, and productivity. This approach is particularly pertinent in knowledge-based industries where creativity and innovation are key.

Education: Educational systems are evolving to address not just cognitive development but also emotional and social needs, aligning with Maslow's principles. There's a growing emphasis on holistic education that supports students' well-being and self-actualization, preparing them to navigate the complexities of the 21st century.

Social Policy and Humanitarian Efforts: As global challenges such as poverty, inequality, and refugee crises persist, Maslow's hierarchy informs social policies aimed at meeting basic human needs as a foundation for stable, prosperous societies. This perspective is critical in humanitarian efforts, where addressing physiological and safety needs is the first step toward recovery and development.

Technology and Social Media: The digital age has introduced complex dynamics in how social and esteem needs are met, with social media playing a significant role in influencing individuals' sense of belonging and self-esteem. Maslow's framework offers a lens through which to understand the psychological impacts of digital connectedness and the quest for validation in virtual communities.

Environmental Sustainability: The growing awareness of environmental sustainability reflects a collective movement towards Maslow's higher values of self-actualization and transcendence, recognizing the interconnectedness of all life and the importance of acting beyond self-interest for the well-being of the planet.

Life of Abraham Maslow

Dr. Abraham Maslow, born on April 1, 1908, in Brooklyn, New York, emerged as one of the most influential psychologists of the twentieth century, renowned for his pioneering work in humanistic psychology. His journey into psychology began at the University of Wisconsin, where he initially embarked on the study of law to satisfy his parents' wishes but soon found his passion in psychology, earning his BA in 1930, his MA in 1931, and his PhD in 1934 (Hoffman, 1988).

Maslow's early academic career included working with Harry

Harlow, famous for his research with rhesus monkeys and attachment behavior, which profoundly influenced Maslow's thinking about human needs and motivation (Maslow, 1943). After his doctoral work, Maslow returned to New York, engaging in research at Columbia University where he encountered cultural anthropologist Ruth Benedict and Gestalt psychologist Max Wertheimer, whose ideas greatly influenced his psychological perspective, leading him to focus on the potentialities and positive aspects of human nature (Hoffman, 1988).

Throughout his career, Maslow sought to understand what drives human beings, leading to the development of his Hierarchy of Needs, a theory that proposed humans are motivated by a progression of needs, culminating in self-actualization. Unlike many of his contemporaries who focused on pathology, Maslow was more interested in human potential, well-being, and the factors that contribute to achieving a fulfilled life (Maslow, 1954).

Maslow's tenure at Brandeis University from 1951 until his death in 1970 marked the period of his most significant contributions. It was here that he became the chair of the psychology department, further developing his theories on self-actualization and the hierarchy of needs (Maslow, 1968). His work extended beyond psychology to influence fields such as business management, education, and even the emerging field of positive psychology, emphasizing the importance of focusing on strengths and virtues (Maslow, 1971).

Maslow was not without his critics, some of whom argued that his theory was too idealistic and not universally applicable across different cultural contexts. Despite these criticisms, Maslow's optimistic view of humanity has endured, offering a counterpoint to the more deterministic perspectives prevalent in psychology at the time (Hofstede, 1984).

Dr. Abraham Maslow passed away on June 8, 1970, leaving behind a legacy that continues to influence psychology and many other disciplines. His work remains a testament to the belief in the goodness of human beings and their inherent drive towards growth, freedom, and fulfillment.

Biology and Behavior

Dr. Robert Sapolsky, PhD (21st Century)

Front:
  Topic: Biology & Behavior
  Key Figure: Dr. R. Sapolsky
  Focus: Link between biological processes & behavior.

Back:
  Insights:
  Stress impacts health/behavior.
  Evolution influences social dynamics.
  Relevance:Mental health treatments.
  Understanding social behavior.Critiques: Need for broader
sociocultural integration.

Simple Definition of Biology and Behavior

Biology and behavior explores the intricate relationship between biological processes and behavioral patterns, emphasizing how physiological mechanisms, genetics, and environmental factors interact to shape behavior.

Expanded Definition and Context

Dr. Robert Sapolsky, a renowned neuroscientist and biologist, has significantly contributed to our understanding of the biological underpinnings of behavior. His work spans various disciplines, including neurology, endocrinology, and primatology, to provide a comprehensive view of how biological factors influence behavior (Sapolsky, 2004).

Stress and Its Biological Underpinnings: Sapolsky's research on stress, particularly the role of glucocorticoids (stress hormones), has shed light on how prolonged stress affects health and behavior. His studies have demonstrated the complex effects of stress on the brain and body, influencing everything from decision-making to immune function (Sapolsky, 1994).

The Biology of Aggression: Through his work with baboons and other primates, Sapolsky has explored the biological roots of aggression and social hierarchies, illustrating how environmental and hormonal factors contribute to aggressive behaviors (Sapolsky, 2005).

Neuroscience of Human Behavior: Sapolsky has applied insights from primate behavior to understand human behavioral patterns, including the neurological basis of personality, the impact of stress and hormones on behavior, and the biological factors underlying conditions such as depression and aggression (Sapolsky, 2017).

21st Century Applications and Impact

Dr. Robert Sapolsky's contributions to understanding the biological underpinnings of behavior have profound implications for various aspects of 21st-century life and society. His interdisciplinary research offers valuable insights into addressing some of the most pressing challenges of our time.

Mental Health and Neurological Disorders: Sapolsky's exploration of stress and its effects on the brain has revolutionized our approach to mental health, emphasizing the need for holistic treatments that consider both biological and environmental factors. His work supports the development of targeted therapies for stress-related disorders, such as PTSD and depression, by understanding the neurochemical pathways involved (Sapolsky, 2004).

Criminal Justice and Rehabilitation: Insights from Sapolsky's research on aggression and the neurological underpinnings of behavior have significant implications for the criminal justice system. By recognizing the complex interplay of genetics, environment, and neurobiology in shaping behavior, there is a push towards more rehabilitative and less punitive approaches, focusing on addressing the root causes of criminal behavior (Sapolsky, 2017).

Education and Development: Understanding the impact of stress hormones on learning and memory, as elucidated by Sapolsky, has informed educational strategies that aim to create supportive learning environments. This includes recognizing the importance of early childhood environments in shaping lifelong patterns of behavior and learning (Sapolsky, 1994).

Public Health and Policy: Sapolsky's work underscores the importance of addressing socio-economic determinants of health, particularly the role of chronic stress in exacerbating health disparities. This perspective encourages policies that aim to reduce stressors associated with poverty, inequality, and social exclusion, thereby improving overall public health outcomes (Sapolsky, 2004).

Social Cohesion and Conflict Resolution: By shedding light on the biological bases of empathy, cooperation, and aggression, Sapolsky's research offers pathways towards fostering social cohesion and resolving conflicts. His findings suggest strategies for mitigating intergroup conflict and promoting prosocial behavior, essential for navigating the complexities of an increasingly interconnected world (Sapolsky, 2005).

Environmental Sustainability: The application of Sapolsky's research extends to understanding human behavior in the context of environmental conservation. Recognizing the biological and psychological factors that influence environmental attitudes and behaviors can inform more effective strategies for promoting sustainability and addressing climate change (Sapolsky, 2017).

Critiques and Contemporary Views

While Sapolsky's work is widely respected, some debates arise around the determinism of biology in shaping behavior, with critics emphasizing the role of free will and cultural factors. Despite these discussions, Sapolsky's contributions underscore the importance of a multidisciplinary perspective in understanding human behavior (Sapolsky, 2017).

Dr. Robert Sapolsky stands as a pivotal figure in modern science, bridging the gap between biology and psychology. His work not only enriches our understanding of the biological bases of behavior but also encourages a more compassionate view of human nature, considering the myriad influences that shape our actions and interactions.

Personality Assessment

Personality assessment stands as a cornerstone in the quest to unravel the complexities of the human psyche. Far from pigeonholing individuals, it offers a rich, nuanced exploration of the traits and tendencies that constitute the essence of who we are. This exploration is not merely academic; it is profoundly personal and deeply impactful, providing insights that can guide therapeutic interventions, personal growth, and understanding across a spectrum of human experiences (Groth-Marnat, 2009).

The Arsenal of Assessment

Among the myriad tools at our disposal, each serves a unique purpose in painting a detailed picture of human personality. The Rorschach Inkblot Test, for instance, offers a glimpse into the subconscious, inviting interpretations that reveal deeper emotional states and conflicts (Rorschach, 1921). The Minnesota Multiphasic Personality Inventory (MMPI), with its comprehensive scope, assesses a range of psychological conditions, offering a window into the multifaceted nature of human personality (Hathaway & McKinley, 1943). The NEO Personality Inventory (NEO PI-R) navigates through the Big Five personality traits, providing a structured understanding of individual differences in a universally applicable manner (Costa & McCrae, 1992).

The Myers-Briggs Type Indicator (MBTI)

The Myers-Briggs Type Indicator (MBTI) is a personality assessment tool designed to measure psychological preferences in how people perceive the world and make decisions. Based on the typological theory proposed by Carl Jung, the MBTI was developed by Isabel Briggs Myers and her mother, Katharine Cook Briggs, in the early to mid-20th century (Myers & Briggs, 1976). The MBTI categorizes individuals into 16 distinct personality types based on four dichotomies:

1. Extraversion (E) vs. Introversion (I): This dimension assesses where an individual primarily directs their energy—towards the external world or their internal world.
2. Sensing (S) vs. Intuition (N): This measures the preference in the type of information an individual trusts more—concrete, tangible data (Sensing) or abstract, conceptual information (Intuition).
3. Thinking (T) vs. Feeling (F): This dichotomy looks at decision-making preferences, whether an individual tends to prioritize logic and objectivity (Thinking) or personal values and emotions (Feeling).
4. Judging (J) vs. Perceiving (P): This assesses an individual's approach to structure in their life, with Judging indicating a preference for planned, organized environments and Perceiving a more flexible, adaptable approach.
5. The MBTI has been widely used in various settings,

including organizational development, career counseling, and personal growth, to help individuals understand their personality type and how it influences their interactions with others and decision-making processes (Myers, McCaulley, Quenk, & Hammer, 1998).

Despite its popularity, the MBTI has faced criticism from the academic community regarding its validity and reliability. Critics argue that the dichotomous nature of its scales does not account for the complexity and fluidity of personality traits (Pittenger, 1993). Additionally, the stability of type classifications over time and the instrument's predictive utility in professional settings have been questioned.

Nonetheless, the MBTI continues to be a tool of interest for many, offering insights into personal development and team dynamics by fostering a deeper understanding of diverse personality types and promoting appreciation for differing perspectives and approaches (Myers et al., 1998).

Rorschach Inkblot Test

The Rorschach Inkblot Test, developed by Swiss psychiatrist Hermann Rorschach in the early 20th century, remains one of the most intriguing and widely discussed psychological assessments. This projective test involves presenting individuals with a series of inkblots and asking them to describe what they see. The theory behind the test is that people will project their own unconscious thoughts and feelings onto the ambiguous images, thereby revealing underlying aspects of their personality (Rorschach, 1921).

Components and Application

The test consists of 10 inkblots, some in black and white, others incorporating colors. The responses are analyzed based on several dimensions, including the content of what the test-taker sees, the location of the image they focus on, and the determinants, such as form, color, and movement, that influenced their perception. This analysis aims to glean insights into the individual's emotional functioning, personality characteristics, and, in some cases, psychological disorders (Exner, 2003).

Clinical and Psychological Insights

The Rorschach Test has been applied in clinical settings to assist in diagnosing mental health conditions, understanding personality structure, and guiding treatment planning. Its value lies in its ability to elicit responses that might not emerge through more structured assessments, providing a unique window into the psyche (Exner, 2003).

Debates and Criticisms

Despite its longstanding use, the Rorschach Inkblot Test has been the subject of considerable debate within the psychological community. Criticisms often focus on issues of validity, reliability, and the subjective nature of interpreting responses. Proponents argue that when administered and interpreted by trained professionals, using standardized scoring systems like the Exner Comprehensive System, the test can offer valuable clinical insights (Wood, Nezworski, Lilienfeld, & Garb, 2003).

Contemporary Relevance

In modern psychological practice, the Rorschach Inkblot Test is often used alongside other assessment tools to provide a more comprehensive view of an individual's psychological profile. It continues to fascinate both clinicians and the public, serving as a testament to the complexity of human perception and personality.

The Thematic Apperception Test (TAT)

The Thematic Apperception Test (TAT), developed by psychologist Henry A. Murray in the 1930s, is a projective psychological test designed to uncover the underlying motives, concerns, and the way individuals view the social world through the stories they narrate in response to ambiguous pictures. Unlike more structured questionnaires, the TAT offers a unique window into the personal world of individuals, revealing aspects of personality that are difficult to measure directly (Murray, 1943).

Methodology and Interpretation

The TAT consists of a series of ambiguous images depicting various social and interpersonal situations. Test takers are asked to create a story for each image, including what led up to the scene, what is happening at the moment, what the characters are feeling and thinking, and how the situation might resolve. The responses are believed to reflect the test taker's own experiences, projections, and internal conflicts, rather than the content of the pictures themselves. Psychologists interpret these narratives to gain insights into a person's social drives, needs, emotions, and patterns of response to complex situations (Morgan & Murray, 1935).

Applications of the TAT

The TAT has been used in a wide range of settings, including clinical psychology, research, and occupational testing. In clinical practice, it helps therapists understand clients' unresolved conflicts, dominant drives, emotions, and complex relational patterns. The TAT is also used in personality research to explore themes such as achievement motivation, power dynamics, and attachment styles. In occupational settings, it can assist in evaluating individuals' suitability for certain roles, based on their motivations and interpersonal orientation (Cramer, 1999).

Critiques and Considerations

Despite its longstanding use, the TAT has faced criticism regarding its reliability and validity. The subjective nature of story interpretation can lead to significant variability between examiners, raising concerns about the objectivity of the insights derived from the test. Moreover, the lack of standardized scoring systems has been a point of contention, although some standardized approaches have been developed (Cramer, 1999). Proponents argue that the rich qualitative data obtained from the TAT offer valuable perspectives on personality that are not easily captured by more structured assessments.

Contemporary Relevance

The TAT remains a valuable tool within psychology, particularly for exploring deep-seated emotional issues and interpersonal dynamics. Its utility lies in its ability to prompt self-reflection and reveal aspects of personality below the surface of conscious awareness. As with all projective tests, the TAT is most effective when used as part of a broader assessment battery, integrating its findings with other sources of psychological data to provide a comprehensive view of an individual's personality (Murray, 1943; Cramer, 1999).

Implications in the Modern World

In an era where the significance of mental health is increasingly recognized, the role of personality assessment transcends academic boundaries. These tools are instrumental in devising personalized treatment plans, enhancing self-awareness, and facilitating healthier workplace dynamics. They empower us to confront the challenges of life with a deeper understanding of our inner workings, promoting resilience and adaptability (Butcher, Mineka, & Hooley, 2014).

The significance of personality assessment in contemporary society extends well beyond the confines of academic research, touching virtually every aspect of human life. As we navigate an era marked by a growing acknowledgment of mental health's importance, the applications of these tools unfold in diverse and impactful ways, reshaping therapeutic practices, personal development, and organizational culture.

Personalized Therapeutic Approaches

One of the most profound implications lies in the realm of mental health treatment. Personality assessments provide clinicians with nuanced insights into their clients' psychological landscapes, enabling the development of tailored therapeutic strategies that address specific needs and conditions. By understanding the underlying personality traits that contribute to or exacerbate mental health issues, practitioners can apply interventions more effectively, improving outcomes for individuals grappling with psychological disorders (Butcher, Mineka, & Hooley, 2014).

Enhancement of Self-Awareness and Personal Growth

Beyond clinical settings, personality assessments serve as powerful tools for personal growth and self-exploration. They offer individuals a framework to understand their behaviors, preferences, and emotional responses, fostering a deeper level of self-awareness. This introspection can lead to greater self-acceptance, improved relationship dynamics, and a more conscious approach to life's decisions. By illuminating the strengths and potential areas for development, these assessments empower individuals to pursue personal and professional growth with clarity and confidence.

Workplace Dynamics and Organizational Development

In organizational contexts, personality assessments contribute to creating harmonious and productive work environments. They assist in team formation, leadership development, and conflict resolution by highlighting the diverse personality types and how they can best interact. Understanding employees' personality traits can lead to more effective communication, enhanced team cohesion, and increased job satisfaction. Moreover, these insights can inform hiring decisions, ensuring that individuals' roles align with their strengths and preferences, thereby optimizing organizational effectiveness and employee well-being.

Promoting Resilience and Adaptability

At a broader societal level, the insights gained from personality assessments underscore the importance of resilience and adaptability. By fostering an understanding of one's personality traits, individuals can develop strategies to manage stress, navigate change, and overcome challenges more effectively. This awareness can lead to healthier coping mechanisms, a more adaptable outlook on life, and the resilience needed to face the uncertainties of the modern world.

Ethical Considerations and Future Directions

The practice of personality assessment is laden with ethical responsibilities. The interpretation and application of assessment outcomes require a delicate balance, ensuring respect for individual dignity and confidentiality. As we move forward, the field of personality assessment continues to evolve, integrating technological advancements and new research findings. The future promises even more sophisticated tools that will deepen our understanding of the human psyche, always with the caveat of navigating the ethical complexities inherent in this deeply personal area of study (Butcher, Mineka, & Hooley, 2014).

Some Thoughts

The journey into the realm of personality assessment represents far more than a mere academic exercise; it embodies our profound and perpetual intrigue with the essence of human existence. This endeavor marries the precision of scientific exploration with the nuanced artistry of comprehending both oneself and those around us. As we navigate through the intricacies of personality tests and the theories that underpin them, we're invited into a deeper appreciation of the human spirit's complexity.

This process of exploration does not merely catalog traits or categorize individuals into simplistic types; instead, it opens up avenues for empathy, self-discovery, and a more compassionate understanding of the diverse tapestries that make up human personalities. It challenges us to consider the myriad factors that influence who we are—from the genetic blueprints that shape our tendencies to the environmental contexts that mold our experiences and choices.

Moreover, the study of personality and its assessment brings to light the incredible capacity for change and adaptation that defines the human experience. It underscores the notion that our personalities are not fixed entities but are fluid and evolving, shaped by our decisions, experiences, and the relationships we forge. This realization empowers us to take an active role in our personal development, encouraging a mindset of growth and an openness to the transformative power of self-awareness.

In essence, the exploration of personality through assessment serves as a profound reminder of our shared humanity. It highlights the beauty of our differences, the complexity of our inner worlds, and the unending potential each person holds for insight, change, and connection. As we continue to delve into the mysteries of the human psyche, let us do so with curiosity, compassion, and an unwavering commitment to understanding the depths of what it truly means to be human.

Personality in Everyday Life

Introduction to Personality in Daily Contexts

Personality permeates every facet of our daily lives, influencing how we think, feel, and interact with the world around us. It shapes our perceptions, guides our decisions, and affects our relationships. This chapter explores the practical implications of personality traits in various aspects of everyday life, from personal growth and interpersonal relationships to career success and social interactions.

Personality and Interpersonal Relationships

At the heart of social life, personality traits play a pivotal role in shaping the quality and dynamics of our relationships. For instance, individuals high in agreeableness tend to have more harmonious relationships, while those high in neuroticism may experience more conflict and less satisfaction in their relation-ships (Graziano & Tobin, 2009). Understanding the influence of personality can lead to more empathetic interactions and effective communication strategies, enhancing relational well-being.

Personality in the Workplace

In the workplace, personality traits contribute to job performance, leadership styles, and team dynamics. The Big Five personality traits, including conscientiousness and emotional stability, are predictive of job performance across various occupations (Barrick & Mount, 1991). Additionally, personality assessments are increasingly used in organizational settings to inform hiring decisions, team building, and leadership development programs, aiming to optimize workplace efficiency and culture.

Adaptation and Personal Growth

Personality is not static; it reflects a dynamic interplay between inherent traits and life experiences. This adaptability is crucial for personal growth and coping with life's challenges. For example, openness to experience is associated with flexibility and creativity, aiding adaptation to change (McCrae & Costa, 2003). Recognizing and leveraging one's personality traits can facilitate resilience, goal achievement, and overall personal development.

Lifestyle Choices and Health Behaviors

Personality traits also influence lifestyle choices and health behaviors. Conscientious individuals are more likely to engage in health-promoting behaviors and have better health outcomes, while high levels of neuroticism are linked to stress-related health issues (Bogg & Roberts, 2004). Awareness of these patterns can motivate proactive health management and lifestyle adjustments.

The Ubiquity of Personality

Personality in everyday life underscores the ubiquity and significance of personality traits in shaping human experience. From enhancing personal relationships to navigating the complexities of the workplace, understanding personality offers valuable insights into human behavior and potential. As we continue to explore the nuances of personality, we open doors to improved self-awareness, more fulfilling interactions, and a deeper appreciation of the diversity that defines the human condition.

Bibliography

Angell, J. R. (1907). The province of functional psychology. Psychological Review, 14(2), 61-91.

Asch, S. E. (1955). Opinions and social pressure. Scientific American, 193(5), 31-35.

Asch, S. E. (1956). Studies of independence and conformity: A minority of one against a unanimous majority. Psychological Monographs: General and Applied, 70(9), 1-70.

Bandura, A. (1977). Social Learning Theory. Prentice Hall.

Bandura, A. (1986). Social Foundations of Thought and Action: A Social Cognitive Theory. Prentice-Hall.

Bandura, A., Ross, D., & Ross, S. A. (1961). Transmission of aggression through imitation of aggressive models. Journal of Abnormal and Social Psychology, 63(3), 575-582.

Bagozzi, R. P., Gopinath, M., & Nyer, P. U. (1999). The role of emotions in marketing. Journal of the Academy of Marketing Science, 27(2), 184-206.

Baumrind, D. (1964). Some thoughts on ethics of research: After reading Milgram's "Behavioral Study of Obedience." American Psychologist, 19(6), 421-423.

Beck, A. T. (1963). Thinking and depression: Idiosyncratic content and cognitive distortions. Archives of General Psychiatry, 9(4), 324-333.

Beck, A. T. (1964). Thinking and depression: Theory and therapy. Archives of General Psychiatry, 10, 561-571.

Beck, A. T. (1979). Cognitive Therapy and the Emotional Disorders. Meridian.

Beck, A. T., Rush, A. J., Shaw, B. F., & Emery, G. (1979). Cognitive Therapy of Depression. John Wiley & Sons.

Bellizzi, J. A., & Hite, R. E. (1992). Environmental color, consumer feelings, and purchase likelihood. Psychology & Marketing, 9(5), 347-363.

Boring, E. G. (1950). A History of Experimental Psychology (2nd ed.). Appleton-Century-Crofts.

Bogg, T., & Roberts, B. W. (2004). Conscientiousness and health-related behaviors: A meta-analysis of the leading behavioral contributors to mortality. Psychological Bulletin, 130(6), 887-919.

Bjork, D. W. (1993). B.F. Skinner: A Life. American Psychological Association.

Binet, A., & Simon, T. (1905). Méthodes nouvelles pour le diagnostic du niveau intellectuel des anormaux. L'Année Psychologique.

Blumenthal, A. L. (1970). Language and psychology: Historical aspects of psycholinguistics. Wiley.

Buckley, K. W. (1989). Mechanical Man: John Broadus Watson and the Beginnings of Behaviorism. Guilford Press.

Butcher, J. N., Mineka, S., & Hooley, J. M. (2014). Abnormal Psychology. Pearson.

Cattell, R. B. (1946). The description and measurement of personality. Yonkers-on-Hudson, NY: World Book.

Cattell, R. B., Eber, H. W., & Tatsuoka, M. M. (1970). Handbook for the Sixteen Personality Factor Questionnaire (16PF). Champaign, IL: Institute for Personality and Ability Testing.

Chomsky, N. (1959). Review of Verbal Behavior by B.F. Skinner. Language, 35(1), 26-58.

Clark, D. A. (2013). Cognitive restructuring. In O. J. D. & T. L. C. (Eds.), The Wiley Handbook of Cognitive Behavioral Therapy (pp. 1-22). Wiley-Blackwell.

Costa, P. T., & McCrae, R. R. (1985). The NEO Personality Inventory manual. Psychological Assessment Resources.

Costa, P. T., & McCrae, R. R. (1992). Revised NEO Personality Inventory (NEO PI-R) and NEO Five-Factor Inventory (NEO-FFI) professional manual. Psychological Assessment Resources.

Côté, J. E., & Levine, C. (2002). Identity Formation, Agency, and Culture: A Social Psychological Synthesis. Lawrence Erlbaum Associates.

Craske, M. G., Kircanski, K., Zelikowsky, M., Mystkowski, J., Chowdhury, N., & Baker, A. (2009). Optimizing inhibitory learning during exposure therapy. Behaviour Research and Therapy, 47(1), 5-27.

Cramer, P. (1999). Using the TAT to assess the relation between gender identity and the use of defense mechanisms. Journal of Personality Assessment, 73(1), 169-188.

Deci, E. L. (1971). Effects of Externally Mediated Rewards on Intrinsic Motivation. Journal of Personality and Social Psychology, 18(1), 105-115.

Durkheim, É. (1897). Suicide: A Study in Sociology. Free Press.

Erikson, E. H. (1950). Childhood and Society. Norton.

Erikson, E. H. (1959). Identity and the Life Cycle. International Universities Press.

Erikson, E. H. (1963). Youth: Change and Challenge. Basic Books.

Erikson, E. H. (1968). Identity: Youth and Crisis. Norton.

Eysenck, H. J. (1947). Dimensions of Personality. Routledge & Kegan Paul.

Eysenck, H. J. (1970). The Structure of Human Personality. Methuen.

Farah, M. J. (2012). Neuroethics: An Introduction with Readings. MIT Press.

Ferguson, C. J., & Kilburn, J. (2009). The Public Health Risks of Media Violence: A Meta-Analytic Review. The Journal of Pediatrics, 154(5), 759-763.

Frankl, V. E. (1946). Man's Search for Meaning. Beacon Press.

Frankl, V. E. (1959). The Will to Meaning: Foundations and Applications of Logotherapy. Plume.

Freud, S. (1894). The Neuro-psychoses of Defence. SE, 3: 45-61.

Freud, S. (1895). Studies on Hysteria. SE, 2.

Freud, S. (1900). The Interpretation of Dreams. SE, 4-5.

Freud, S. (1905). Three Essays on the Theory of Sexuality. SE, 7: 125-243.

Freud, S. (1915). Repression. SE, 14: 146-158.

Freud, S. (1917). Introductory Lectures on Psychoanalysis. SE, 15-16.

Freud, S. (1920). Beyond the Pleasure Principle. SE, 18: 7-64.

Freud, S. (1921). Group Psychology and the Analysis of the Ego. SE, 18: 65-143.

Freud, S. (1923). The Ego and the Id. SE, 19: 12-66.

Freud, S. (1927). The Future of an Illusion. SE, 21: 1-56.

Freud, S. (1930). Civilization and Its Discontents. SE, 21: 59-145.

Friedman, L. J. (1999). Identity's Architect: A Biography of Erik H. Erikson. Scribner.

Gardner, H. (1983). Frames of mind: The theory of multiple

intelligences. Basic Books.

Gay, P. (1988). Freud: A Life for Our Time. W. W. Norton & Company.

Ghaemi, S. N. (2009). The rise and fall of the biopsychosocial model. The British Journal of Psychiatry, 195(1), 3-4.

Gorn, G. J. (1982). The effects of music in advertising on choice behavior: A classical conditioning approach. Journal of Marketing, 46(1), 94-101.

Groth-Marnat, G. (2009). Handbook of Psychological Assessment. John Wiley & Sons.

Grünbaum, A. (1984). The Foundations of Psychoanalysis: A Philosophical Critique. University of California Press.

Haidt, J. (2001). The Emotional Dog and Its Rational Tail: A Social Intuitionist Approach to Moral Judgment. Psychological Review, 108(4), 814-834.

Harris, B. (1979). Whatever happened to Little Albert? American Psychologist, 34(2), 151-160.

Hathaway, S. R., & McKinley, J. C. (1943). The Minnesota Multiphasic Personality Inventory. University of Minnesota Press.

Hearst, E. (1991). Psychology and nothing. American Scientist, 79(5), 432-443.

Horney, K. (1945). Our Inner Conflicts: A Constructive Theory of Neurosis. W. W. Norton & Company.

Horney, K. (1950). Neurosis and Human Growth: The Struggle Towards Self-Realization. W. W. Norton & Company.

Horney, K. (1967). Feminine Psychology. W. W. Norton & Company.

Hofstede, G. (1984). Cultural dimensions in management and planning. Asia Pacific Journal of Management, 1(2), 81-99.

Hoffman, E. (1988). The Right to Be Human: A Biography of

Abraham Maslow. McGraw-Hill.

James, W. (1890). Principles of Psychology. Henry Holt and Company.

Jung, C. G. (1912). Psychology of the Unconscious. Moffat, Yard and Company.

Jung, C. G. (1959). Archetypes and the Collective Unconscious. Princeton University Press.

Jung, C. G. (1960). Synchronicity: An Acausal Connecting Principle. Princeton University Press.

Jung, C. G. (1964). Man and His Symbols. Dell.

Jung, C. G. (1966). Two Essays on Analytical Psychology. Princeton University Press.

Jung, C. G. (1974). Dreams. Princeton University Press.

Jung, C. G., & Freud, S. (1974). The Freud/Jung Letters. Princeton University Press.

Kahneman, D., & Tversky, A. (1979). Prospect Theory: An Analysis of Decision under Risk. Econometrica, 47(2), 263-291.

Kandel, E. R. (2001). The molecular biology of memory storage: A dialogue between genes and synapses. Science, 294(5544), 1030-1038.

Kazdin, A. E. (1982). The Token Economy: A Decade Later. Journal of Applied Behavior Analysis, 15(3), 431-445.

Kelly, G. A. (1955). The Psychology of Personal Constructs. New York: Norton.

Keller, K. L. (1987). Memory factors in advertising: The effect of advertising retrieval cues on brand evaluations. Journal of Consumer Research, 14(3), 316-333.

Kerr, J. (1994). A Most Dangerous Method: The Story of Jung, Freud, and Sabina Spielrein. Knopf.

Kroger, J., & Marcia, J. E. (2011). The identity statuses: Origins, meanings, and interpretations. In Schwartz, S. J.,

Luyckx, K., & Vignoles, V. L. (Eds.), Handbook of identity theory and research. Springer.

Leahey, T. H. (1992). The Mythical Revolutions of American Psychology. American Psychologist, 47(2), 308-318.

Lewin, K. (1936). Principles of Topological Psychology. McGraw-Hill.

Lewin, K. (1947). Frontiers in Group Dynamics: Concept, Method and Reality in Social Science; Social Equilibria and Social Change. Human Relations, 1(1), 5-41.

Lewin, K. (1948). Resolving Social Conflicts; Selected Papers on Group Dynamics. G. W. Lewin (ed.). Harper & Row.

Lewin, K. (1951). Field Theory in Social Science: Selected Theoretical Papers. D. Cartwright (ed.). Harper & Row.

Loftus, E. F. (1975). Leading questions and the eyewitness report. Cognitive Psychology, 7(4), 560-572.

Loftus, E. F., & Palmer, J. C. (1974). Reconstruction of automobile destruction: An example of the interaction between language and memory. Journal of Verbal Learning and Verbal Behavior, 13(5), 585-589.

Loftus, E. F., & Pickrell, J. E. (1995). The formation of false memories. Psychiatric Annals, 25(12), 720-725.

Loftus, E. F. (2003). Make-believe memories. American Psychologist, 58(11), 867-873.

Loftus, E. F. (1993). The reality of repressed memories. American Psychologist, 48(5), 518-537.

Maslow, A. H. (1943). A theory of human motivation. Psychological Review, 50(4), 370-396.

Maslow, A. H. (1954). Motivation and Personality. Harper & Row.

Maslow, A. H. (1968). Toward a Psychology of Being. Van Nostrand Reinhold.

Maslow, A. H. (1971). The Farther Reaches of Human Nature. Viking Press.

Masten, A. S., Burt, K. B., & Coatsworth, J. D. (2005). Competence and psychopathology in development. In Cicchetti, D., & Cohen, D. J. (Eds.), Developmental psychopathology: Vol. 3. Risk, disorder, and adaptation. Wiley.

May, R. (1953). Man's Search for Himself. W. W. Norton & Company.

May, R. (1958). The Origins and Significance of the Existential Movement in Psychology. W. W. Norton & Company.

May, R. (1967). Psychology and the Human Dilemma. Van Nostrand.

May, R. (1975). The Courage to Create. W. W. Norton & Company.

May, R. (1983). The Discovery of Being. W. W. Norton & Company.

McCrae, R. R., & Costa, P. T. (1987). Validation of the five-factor model of personality across instruments and observers. Journal of Personality and Social Psychology, 52(1), 81-90.

McCrae, R. R., & John, O. P. (1992). An introduction to the five-factor model and its applications. Journal of Personality, 60(2), 175-215.

McLellan, D. (1997). Marxism and the Interpretations of Culture. Macmillan.

Mead, M. (1935). Sex and Temperament in Three Primitive Societies. William Morrow & Company.

Milgram, S. (1963). Behavioral study of obedience. Journal of Abnormal and Social Psychology, 67(4), 371-378.

Milgram, S. (1967). The small world problem. Psychology Today, 1(1), 61-67.

Miller, G. A. (1956). The magical number seven, plus or minus two: Some limits on our capacity for processing information. Psychological Review, 63(2), 81-97.

Mischel, W. (1968). Personality and Assessment. Wiley.

Morgan, C. D., & Murray, H. A. (1935). A method for investigating fantasies: The Thematic Apperception Test. Archives of Neurology and Psychiatry, 34(2), 289-306.

Morris, W. N., & Miller, R. S. (1975). The effects of consensus-breaking and consensus-preempting partners on reduction in conformity. Journal of Experimental Social Psychology, 11(2), 215-223.

Murray, H. A. (1943). Thematic Apperception Test manual. Harvard University Press.

Myers, I. B., & Briggs, K. C. (1976). The Myers-Briggs Type Indicator. Consulting Psychologists Press.

Myers, I. B., McCaulley, M. H., Quenk, N. L., & Hammer, A. L. (1998). MBTI Manual (A guide to the development and use of the Myers Briggs type indicator). Consulting Psychologists Press.

Neimeyer, G. J., & Neimeyer, R. A. (2003). Advances in Personal Construct Psychology: New Directions and Perspectives. Praeger.

Neimeyer, R. A. (1985). The development of personal construct psychology. University of Nebraska Press.

Neisser, U. (1967). Cognitive Psychology. Appleton-Century-Crofts.

Nisbett, R. E., et al. (2012). Intelligence: New findings and theoretical developments. American Psychologist.

Öhman, A., & Mineka, S. (2001). Fears, phobias, and preparedness: Toward an evolved module of fear and fear learning. Psychological Review, 108(3), 483-522.

Paris, B. J. (1994). Karen Horney: A Psychoanalyst's Search

for Self-Understanding. Yale University Press.

Pavlov, I. P. (1927). Conditioned reflexes: An investigation of the physiological activity of the cerebral cortex. Oxford University Press.

Pelham, W. E., & Fabiano, G. A. (2008). Evidence-based psychosocial treatments for attention-deficit/hyperactivity disorder. Journal of Clinical Child & Adolescent Psychology, 37(1), 184-214.

Piaget, J. (1952). The Origins of Intelligence in Children. International Universities Press.

Piaget, J. (1954). The Construction of Reality in the Child. Basic Books.

Piaget, J. (1970). Science of Education and the Psychology of the Child. Orion Press.

Piaget, J. (1971). Biology and Knowledge: An Essay on the Relations between Organic Regulations and Cognitive Processes. University of Chicago Press.

Piaget, J. (1972). Intellectual Evolution from Adolescence to Adulthood. Human Development, 15(1), 1-12.

Piaget, J. (1985). The Equilibration of Cognitive Structures: The Central Problem of Intellectual Development. University of Chicago Press.

Pinker, S. (2002). The Blank Slate: The Modern Denial of Human Nature. Viking.

Pittenger, D. J. (1993). The utility of the Myers-Briggs Type Indicator. Review of Educational Research, 63(4), 467-488.

Poropat, A. E. (2009). A meta-analysis of the five-factor model of personality and academic performance. Psychological Bulletin, 135(2), 322-338.

Popper, K. (1963). Conjectures and Refutations: The Growth of Scientific Knowledge. Routledge.

Quinn, B. A. (2013). The Karen Horney Clinic: A beacon of hope for the neurotic individual. American Journal of Psychoanalysis, 73(1), 58-66.

Ravenette, A. T. (1998). Personal Construct Theory and Educational Psychology. Educational Psychology in Practice.

Rogers, C. R. (1951). Client-centered Therapy: Its Current Practice, Implications, and Theory. Houghton Mifflin.

Rotter, J. B. (1954). Social learning and clinical psychology. Prentice-Hall.

Rotter, J. B. (1966). Generalized expectancies for internal versus external control of reinforcement. Psychological Monographs: General and Applied, 80(1), 1-28.

Rotter, J. B. (1975). Some problems and misconceptions related to the construct of internal versus external control of reinforcement. Journal of Consulting and Clinical Psychology, 43(1), 56-67.

Rotter, J. B. (1982). The development and applications of social learning theory: Selected papers. Praeger.

Rotter, J. B. (1989). Internal versus external control of reinforcement: A case history of a variable. American Psychologist, 45(4), 489-493.

Rothbaum, B. O., Hodges, L., Smith, S., Lee, J. H., & Price, L. (1995). A controlled study of virtual reality exposure therapy for the fear of flying. Journal of Consulting and Clinical Psychology, 63(6), 1020-1026.

Russell, M. T., & Karol, D. L. (2002). The 16PF Fifth Edition Technical Manual. Champaign, IL: Institute for Personality and Ability Testing.

Ryan, R. M., & Deci, E. L. (2000). Intrinsic and Extrinsic Motivations: Classic Definitions and New Directions. Contemporary Educational Psychology, 25(1), 54-67.

Sapolsky, R. M. (1994). Why zebras don't get ulcers. W.H. Freeman and Company.

Sapolsky, R. M. (2004). The trouble with testosterone: And other essays on the biology of the human predicament. Scribner.

Sapolsky, R. M. (2005). A primate's memoir: A neuroscientist's unconventional life among the baboons. Scribner.

Sapolsky, R. M. (2017). Behave: The biology of humans at our best and worst. Penguin Press.

Samuels, A. (1985). Jung and the Post-Jungians. Routledge & Kegan Paul.

Sch Skinner, B. F. (1938). The Behavior of Organisms: An Experimental Analysis. Appleton-Century.

Skinner, B. F. (1948). Walden Two. Macmillan.

Skinner, B. F. (1953). Science and Human Behavior. Macmillan.

Skinner, B. F. (1957). Verbal Behavior. Appleton-Century-Crofts.

Snyder, C. R., & Lopez, S. J. (2007). Positive Psychology: The Scientific and Practical Explorations of Human Strengths. Sage Publications.

Sternberg, R. J. (1999). Handbook of intelligence. Cambridge University Press.

Sternberg, R. J., & Detterman, D. K. (1986). What is intelligence? Contemporary viewpoints on its nature and definition. Ablex Publishing.

Titchener, E. B. (1901-1905). Experimental Psychology: A Manual of Laboratory Practice. Macmillan.

Todes, D. P. (2002). Pavlov's Physiology Factory. Johns Hopkins University Press.

Vygotsky, L. (1978). Mind in Society: The Development of

Higher Psychological Processes. Harvard University Press.

Watson, J. B. (1913). Psychology as the behaviorist views it. Psychological Review, 20(2), 158-177.

Watson, J. B., & Rayner, R. (1920). Conditioned emotional reactions. Journal of Experimental Psychology, 3(1), 1-14.

Wechsler, D. (1955). Manual for the Wechsler Adult Intelligence Scale. Psychological Corporation.

Webster-Stratton, C., & Reid, M. J. (2003). The Incredible Years Parents, Teachers, and Children Training Series: A multifaceted treatment approach for young children with conduct problems. In A. E. Kazdin & J. R. Weisz (Eds.), Evidence-Based Psychotherapies for Children and Adolescents (pp. 224-240). Guilford Press.

Westkott, M. (1993). The Feminist Legacy of Karen Horney. Yale University Press.

Windholz, G. (1997). Ivan P. Pavlov: An overview of his life and psychological work. American Psychologist, 52(9), 941-946.

Wolpe, J. (1958). Psychotherapy by Reciprocal Inhibition. Stanford University Press.

Wood, J. M., Nezworski, M. T., Lilienfeld, S. O., & Garb, H. N. (2003). What's wrong with the Rorschach? Science confronts the controversial inkblot test. Jossey-Bass.

Yalom, I. D. (1980). Existential Psychotherapy. Basic Books.

Additional Materials and Resources

Books:

"The Road to Character" by David Brooks: Explores the importance of character in personal development, offering insights into how individuals have built strong inner lives.

"Quiet: The Power of Introverts in a World That Can't Stop Talking" by Susan Cain: Delves into the strengths and challenges of being an introvert in today's extroverted society.

"Mindset: The New Psychology of Success" by Carol S. Dweck: Introduces the concept of fixed vs. growth mindsets and their impact on personal and professional growth.

"Personality: What Makes You the Way You Are" by Daniel Nettle: A concise guide to the Big Five personality traits and their influence on behavior and life choices.

Online Courses:

"Introduction to Psychology" (Coursera, offered by Yale University): Provides a broad overview of psychological science, including sections on personality psychology.

"Personality Types at Work" (Udemy): Explores how understanding personality types can improve workplace dynamics and personal career success.

"Psychological First Aid" (Coursera, offered by Johns Hopkins University): Offers insights into understanding and managing emotional responses, which can be influenced by personality.

Other Resources:

TED Talks on Personality: Features speakers from various fields sharing insights on personality, its impact on life, and how we understand ourselves and others. Example talks include Susan Cain's "The Power of Introverts" and Angela Lee Duckworth's "Grit: The Power of Passion and Perseverance."

The Psychology of Personality (YouTube, The School of Life): A series of videos exploring different aspects of personality, including traits, disorders, and the history of personality psychology.

Journals:

"Journal of Personality and Social Psychology": Publishes original papers in all areas of personality and social psychology, with implications for understanding personal dynamics in everyday life.

"Personality and Individual Differences": A journal focusing on research related to personality, individual differences, and how these influence human behavior.

Websites:

Simply Psychology (www.simplypsychology.org/personality.html): Offers articles, resources, and overviews on various personality theories and psychological assessments.

Psychology Today (www.psychologytoday.com/us/basics/personality): Features a wide range of articles on personality, including discussions on personality types, traits, and how personality influences our lives.

About the Author

Adam Ian Stratmeyer's diverse writings reflect a life of genuine exploration and intellectual curiosity. Spanning music, technology, academic achievements in psychology and biology, and a Juris Doctorate, his career includes roles from a short-order cook to a college educator and consultant. His authorial scope encompasses academic resources, children's literature, and scientific explorations, all rooted in kindness and reasoned thought. His unique insights aim to illuminate, entertain, and instill appreciation for the wonders of existence. His writing serves as a vibrant tapestry of experiences and knowledge, weaving together the threads of varied passions and expertise. Each piece showcases a profound depth of understanding and a profound love for humanity and the world we inhabit. From profound musings on the human condition to uplifting tales for young minds, Adam's literary universe is an enchanting blend of erudition and heartfelt storytelling, inviting readers of all ages to embark on a journey of discovery and enlightenment.

You can connect with me on:

- https://stratmeyer.wixsite.com/adam-stratmeyer
- https://twitter.com/AdamStratmeyer
- https://adamstratmeyerrethinkingnorms.wordpress.com

Also by Adam Stratmeyer

ODD*': {/'USER*:/TFR*}
The chapters in the book delve into various philosophical and scientific themes, such as the nature of consciousness, the role of language in shaping intelligence, the ethical considerations surrounding AI, and the potential future of human-AI collaboration. The discussion often circles back to the concepts of consciousness, experience, and the philosophical implications of AI in society.

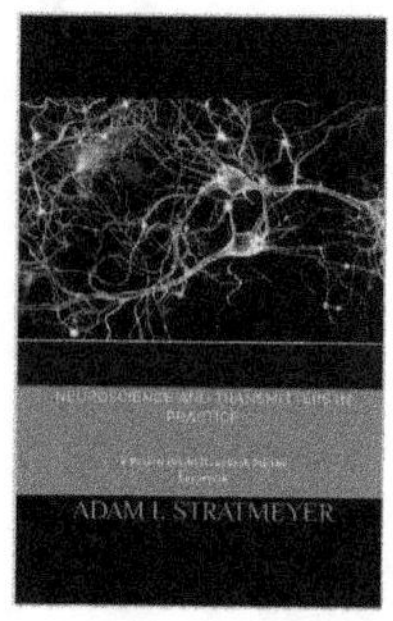

Neuroscience and Transmitters in Practice: A Practical(ish) Handbook for the Layperson
Ever wondered how your brain communicates? Or why certain foods make you feel a certain way? Dive deep into the world of neurotransmitters and discover the intricate dance of chemicals that shape every thought, emotion, and action!

www.ingramcontent.com/pod-product-compliance
Lightning Source LLC
Chambersburg PA
CBHW050803260726
48660CB00004B/1228